Department
for Transport

GW00503774

Know Your
TRAFFIC
SIGNS

Official edition

London: TSO

Department for Transport
Great Minster House
33 Horseferry Road
London SW1P 4DR
Telephone: 0300 330 3000
Website: www.gov.uk/dft

ISBN 978 0 11 554113 1

First published 1975

Sixth edition 2023

Available from tsoshop.co.uk

SD000063

Contents

Introduction

Why know your traffic signs?

Traffic signs play a vital role in directing, informing and controlling road users' behaviour in an effort to make the roads as safe as possible for everyone. This makes a knowledge of traffic signs essential. Not just for new drivers or riders needing to pass their theory test, but for all road users, including experienced professional drivers.

This book aims to illustrate and explain the most common traffic signs that the road user is likely to encounter and is an accompaniment to The Highway Code.

Keeping up to date

We live in times of change. Society, technology and the economy all play their part in changing the way we travel. New traffic signs conveying new messages and in new formats are introduced from time to time, so all drivers and riders need to keep up to date or run the risk of failing to understand or comply with recently introduced signs.

A few examples of events that called for new signs include:

- Britain's first motorway
- air quality zones
- the reintroduction of trams
- advance stop lines
- vehicle-activated signs
- road-charging schemes.

Having experience is all very well, but it's not enough if your knowledge is out of date.

Responsibility for traffic signs

Responsibility for the road network in the UK is split among:

- National Highways in England
- the Welsh Government in Wales
- the Scottish Government in Scotland
- the Department for Infrastructure in Northern Ireland
- local or regional highway authorities.

The central administrations above are responsible for the UK's strategic road network. Strategic roads are the highways that link cities, areas of population, ports and airports. Most motorways and some 'A' roads are strategic roads.

Local or regional highway authorities are responsible for local roads, and this includes a few motorways, all other 'A' roads and all other public roads. While responsibility for placing, erecting and maintaining traffic signs is split among these bodies, it is important that signs are consistent both in appearance and in the way they are used.

To ensure that the UK has a uniform traffic signing system, signs must conform to the designs prescribed in the Traffic Signs Regulations and General Directions 2016 (as amended) (TSRGD) or the equivalent in the devolved administrations, although some signs may have been specially authorised by the Secretary of State or similar in Scotland, Wales and Northern Ireland.

Traffic signs remain the most effective method of communicating to all road users what they need to know to complete their journey safely, efficiently and within the law.

The design of traffic signs and road markings, and their meanings and permitted variants, are generally similar but can vary in Scotland, Wales and Northern Ireland. You should refer also to the information published in those jurisdictions.

The information in this book should not be taken as a definitive statement of the legislation. In the event of a disparity, TSRGD always takes precedence.

A brief history of traffic signs

It was probably the Romans who first used 'traffic signs' in Britain. They marked off road distances at one thousand paces (about one mile) with stones called 'milliaries'.

Most early signposts were erected by private individuals at their own expense. A law passed in 1697 allowed magistrates to direct that inscribed stones or posts be erected at junctions between highways, but it was not until after the General Turnpike Act 1773 that these 'guide posts' or 'fingerposts' became more common.

During the second half of the nineteenth century, bicycles became more popular. Steep hills and sharp bends were very dangerous for early cyclists, and 'danger' and 'caution' signs were erected at the top of steep hills. Signs showing a skull and crossbones were erected at the most dangerous places. Local authorities and cycling organisations installed an estimated 4000 warning signs.

The year 1896 heralded the era of the motor car, and some motoring associations took up the business of placing signs. The Motor Car Act 1903 made local authorities responsible for placing certain warning and prohibitory signs. The signs were for crossroads, steep hills and dangerous bends. 'A' and 'B' numbering of roads was introduced in 1921, and these numbers were shown on fingerpost-style signs alongside the destination and distance. Town or village name signs and warning signs for schools, level crossings and double bends were introduced at the same time.

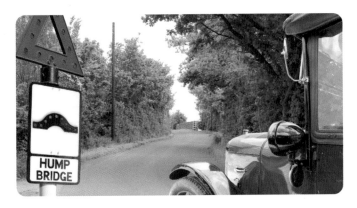

The main task of signposting our roads during the 1920s and 1930s still fell on the motoring organisations, but in 1931 a committee chaired by Sir Henry Maybury was asked to recommend improvements to the signing then in use, and by 1933 further new signs began to appear, including 'No entry' and 'Keep left' signs and warning signs for narrow roads and bridges, low bridges, roundabouts and hospitals. Other signs followed during the 1930s, including 'Halt at major road ahead'. These formed the basis of our traffic signing until the early 1960s.

It was not until after 1918 that white lines began to appear on British roads, and during the 1920s their use spread rapidly. In 1926, the first Ministry of Transport circular on the subject laid down general principles on the use of white lines. In the 1930s, white lines were used as 'stop' lines at road junctions controlled by either police or traffic lights. Reflecting road studs (often referred to as 'cat's eyes') first came into use in 1934. By 1944, white lines were also being used to indicate traffic lanes and define the boundary of the main carriageway at entrances to side roads and lay-bys, and in conjunction with 'halt' signs. In 1959, regulations came into effect to control overtaking by the use of double white lines.

It was realised that the old system of signing would not be adequate for motorways, and the Anderson Committee was set up in 1958 to consider new designs. It recommended much larger signs, with blue backgrounds. Then, in 1961, the Worboys Committee began to review the complete system of traffic signing. It concluded that the UK should adopt the main principles of the European system, with the message expressed as a symbol within a red triangle (for warning signs) or a red circle (for prohibitions). Work began on the conversion of British signs in 1965, and this is still the basic system in use today.

Later developments include the use of yellow box markings at busy road junctions, special signs and road markings at pedestrian crossings, mini-roundabouts and bus lanes. Regulations published in 1994 included new regulatory and warning

signs, and simplified the yellow line system of waiting restrictions that was originally introduced in the 1950s. Further regulations have been published in the period since.

More use is being made of new technology to provide better information to road users on hazards, delays, diversions and traffic control. The future will undoubtedly see more developments in traffic signing to keep pace with the changing traffic demands on our roads.

The signing system

There are three basic types of traffic sign: signs that give orders, signs that warn and signs that give information. Each type has a different shape. A further guide to the function of a sign is its colour. All triangular signs are red.

Circles
give orders

Triangles
warn

Rectangles
inform

Blue circles generally give a mandatory instruction, such as 'turn left', or indicate a route available only to particular classes of traffic, e.g. buses and cycles only

Red rings or circles tell you what you must not do, e.g. you must not exceed 30 mph, no vehicles over the height shown may proceed

Blue rectangles are used for information signs except on motorways, where blue is used for direction signs

Green rectangles are used for direction signs on primary routes

White rectangles are used for direction signs on non-primary routes, or for plates used in combination with warning and regulatory signs

There are a few exceptions to the shape and colour rules, to give certain signs greater prominence. Examples are the 'STOP' and 'GIVE WAY' signs

The words 'must' or 'must not', when used in the descriptions that follow, refer to legal requirements that have to be obeyed.

Warning signs

(other than those for low bridges, railway and tramway level crossings, bus and pedal cycle facilities, traffic calming and road works)

Distance to STOP line

Distance to GIVE WAY line

Traffic signals ahead

Traffic signals that operate only at certain times

Crossroads

T-junction

Side road

Staggered junction

The priority through the junction is indicated by the broader line

Traffic merges from the left

Traffic merges onto main carriageway

Roundabout

Bend to right (left if symbol reversed)

Double bend first to the left (right if symbol reversed)

Junction on a bend (symbols may be reversed)

Plate used with 'roundabout' or 'bend' signs

Adverse camber

Risk of lorries overturning on bend to the left (right if symbol reversed)

Sharp deviation of route to the left (right if chevrons reversed) (alternative designs)

REDUCE SPEED NOW

Plate used with warning signs where a reduction in speed is necessary

Road narrows on both sides

Road narrows on right (left if symbol reversed)

Plates used with 'road narrows' signs

Oncoming vehicles in middle of road

Single file traffic

Single-file traffic in each direction

Single track road

Road wide enough for only one line of vehicles

End of dual carriageway

Two-way traffic

Two-way traffic on route crossing ahead

  Near-side edge of carriageway or obstruction near that edge (alternative shapes). White markers are used on the off-side edge and amber ones on the off-side edge of a dual carriageway

11

Worded warning. 'Ford' may be varied to 'Flood', 'Gate', 'Gates' or 'No smoking'

Try brakes after crossing a ford or before descending a steep hill

Steep hill downwards (10% is equivalent to 1:10)

Steep hill upwards (20% is equivalent to 1:5)

Sign used with 'steep hill' or 'try your brakes' signs

Plates used with 'steep hill' signs

Opening or swing bridge

Quayside or river bank

End of bridge parapet, abutment wall, tunnel mouth etc.

Water course alongside road

Soft verges for distance shown

Tunnel

Hump bridge

Uneven road

Slippery road

Side winds

Distance to hazard

Distance and direction to hazard

Distance over which hazard extends

12

Low-flying
aircraft or
sudden
aircraft noise

Gliders likely

Low-flying
helicopters
or sudden
helicopter
noise

Risk of falling
or fallen rocks

Traffic queues
likely ahead

Slow-moving
military
vehicles likely
to be in or
crossing
the road

Slow-moving
vehicles for
distance shown

Risk of ice.
'Ice' may
be varied to
'Snowdrifts'

Warning of signals
(see page 141).
'FIRE' may be varied
to 'AMBULANCE'
or 'POLICE'

Other danger. The
plate indicates the
nature of the hazard

Zebra or
parallel
crossing

Pedestrians in
road for distance
shown

Frail
pedestrians
likely to cross

Disabled
pedestrians.
'Disabled'
may be varied
to 'Blind'

Children going to or from school

Playground

Patrol

Disabled children

Alternative plates used with 'school' sign

Lights warning of children likely to be crossing the road on their way to or from school (used with 'school' sign)

Pedestrians likely to be crossing a high-speed road where there is no formal crossing point

Horse-drawn vehicles likely to be in the road

Accompanied horses or ponies likely to be in or crossing the road

Wild horses or ponies

Wild animals

Wild fowl

Migratory toad crossing

Sheep

Agricultural vehicles

ANIMAL DISEASE RABIES INFECTED AREA AHEAD

Area infected by animal disease

Pedal cycle
route crossing
or joining the
road ahead

| Child cycle tests | Child cycle training | Cycles crossing | Cycle event |

Plates used with 'cycle route ahead' sign

Part-time advisory
20 mph speed limit
at or near a school

Cattle grid with
indication of
bypass for
horse-drawn
vehicles and
animals

Cattle

Supervised
cattle crossing
ahead

Supervised
cattle crossing

Regulatory signs

(other than those for low bridges, railway and tramway level crossings, bus and pedal cycle facilities and road works)

Most regulatory signs are circular. A **RED RING** or **RED CIRCLE** indicates a prohibition. A **BLUE CIRCLE** generally gives a positive (mandatory) instruction or indicates a route for use only by particular classes of vehicle (see sections on tram signs and bus and cycle signs).

Two notable exceptions are:

The '**STOP**' sign and road markings: you must stop before crossing the transverse line on the road and ensure the way is clear before entering the major road.

(alternative in Wales)

The '**GIVE WAY**' sign and road markings: you must give way to traffic on the major road (the upright sign or both the sign and the triangle on the road might not be used at junctions where there is relatively little traffic).

No entry for vehicular traffic. Where there is an exception for buses or cycles, the sign may be used with a supplementary plate (shown below)

No vehicles except pedal cycles being pushed by hand

Alternative plates used with the 'no vehicles' sign, indicating times when vehicles are prohibited, except for access

No motor vehicles

No motor vehicles except solo motorcycles

No solo motorcycles

No towed caravans

No pedestrians

No ridden or accompanied horses

No horse-drawn vehicles

No articulated vehicles

No goods vehicles over maximum gross weight shown in tonnes

End of goods vehicles restriction

No vehicles carrying explosives

Vehicles carrying dangerous goods with the restriction code indicated by the sign are prohibited from the tunnel. See table for codes that have been assigned to tunnels in the UK.

Tunnel	Category
Dartford	C
Tyne	D
Clyde	D
Mersey	D
Blackwall	E
Limehouse	E
Rotherhithe	E
East India Dock Road	E
Heathrow Airport	Between 4 am and 11 pm: Category E
	At other times: Category C

No vehicles over maximum width shown (width shown in metric and imperial units)

No vehicles or combinations of vehicles over maximum length shown

No vehicles over the maximum gross weight shown in tonnes. The bottom plate is used where empty vehicles are exempt

Plates used to indicate exemptions from prohibition signs

Except for access

Except for access to premises or land adjacent to the road, where there is no other route. Other exemptions may be shown

Except for loading and unloading by goods vehicles

No overtaking

Where a road or bridge is very narrow, priority must be given to traffic from the other direction (there will usually be a 'give way' line indicating where to wait)

Where changes of direction are prohibited, a red bar across the sign is used in addition to the red circle

No U-turn

No right turn

No left turn

A time plate used with a 'no right turn' or 'no left turn' sign indicates a part-time prohibition

Vehicles must not go beyond the sign where displayed by a school crossing patrol

Vehicles must not go beyond the sign where displayed by a police officer or traffic warden

Specified traffic must not use verge maintained in mown or ornamental condition

Proceed in direction indicated by the arrow

Turn left ahead (right if symbol reversed)

Vehicles may pass either side to reach the same destination

Keep left (right if symbol reversed)

Plates
supplementing
'turn' signs

Mini-roundabout
(give way to
traffic from the
immediate right)

One-way
traffic

Vehicles must
not go beyond
the sign where
displayed
during a cycle
event

Nature of and
distance to a
prohibition,
restriction or
requirement

Weight restriction
ahead (may show a
different restriction)

Location of weight
restriction ahead
with indication
of an alternative
route (may show a
different restriction)

Speed limit signs

In areas of street lighting (other than on motorways), a speed limit of 30 mph applies **unless** signs show otherwise. In Wales, this limit is 20 mph.

The maximum speed, in miles per hour, at which traffic may travel, if it is safe to do so

The national speed limit for the type of road and class of traffic applies

A larger sign indicates the start of a speed limit. Smaller repeater signs act as reminders. Repeater signs for a 30 mph limit are used only on roads with no street lighting. Repeater signs for the national speed limit are used only on roads with street lighting (other than motorways)

Road marking used in conjunction with upright signs to indicate the speed limit

Entrance to a 20 mph zone in which traffic-calming measures may be encountered

End of 20 mph zone and start of 30 mph speed limit

Start of a speed limit at the boundary of a town or village

Start of motorway regulations, including the national speed limit (unless a different speed limit is signed)

Point on a road with street lighting where an existing 30 mph limit originally ended but has subsequently been extended (temporary sign). This sign alerts drivers that a previous higher limit has been replaced by a 30 mph limit by the removal of speed limit signs

End of road works and any temporary speed limit through those works (may be supplemented by a sign indicating the permanent speed limit beyond the road works)

Area where speed cameras are in use

Length of road where two cameras are used to measure the average speed of a vehicle between two points

Reminder that enforcement cameras are in use (may be supplemented by a speed limit sign)

Speed camera nearby on a lit road with a 30 mph speed limit (i.e. where there are no speed limit repeater signs)

Speed camera nearby on an unlit road subject to the national speed limit (i.e. where there are no speed limit repeater signs)

Maximum speed advised, in miles per hour, at a bend (the plate may be used with other warning signs)

Minimum speed permitted, in miles per hour, unless it is impracticable or unsafe to comply

End of minimum speed requirement

Start of variable speed limit on a length of road where enforcement cameras are in use

End of variable speed limit. The national speed limit for the type of road and class of traffic now applies

23

Low bridge signs

Each year there are hundreds of incidents in which bridges are struck by vehicles too high to pass under them. Both rail and road users have been killed in these incidents. Look out for signs in this section and **make sure that you are not a bridge basher**.

All bridges with a clearance of less than 16 feet 6 inches (about 5 metres) are normally signed. Both regulatory roundels and warning triangles can be used, depending on the type of bridge.

Bridges particularly at risk from strikes may have a variable message sign that is activated by high vehicles passing through an infra-red beam. When the sign is activated, four amber lights flash, the top pair alternating with the bottom pair.

Regulatory signs

No vehicles over the height shown may pass the sign (height shown in metric and imperial units)

At non-arch bridges mandatory signs may be used; it is unlawful for an overheight vehicle to pass one of these. They are placed on the bridge and at the side of the road in front of the bridge.

Some height restrictions may still show imperial units of measurement only. These signs will be replaced when they reach the end of their life.

Advance warning of a mandatory height restriction ahead; the sign may include an arrow, if the restriction is on a side road

Location of mandatory height restriction ahead, with indication of an alternative route

Warning signs

A warning sign indicates the maximum headroom under a bridge or other overhead obstruction, in metric and imperial units. This sign may be sited well in advance of a bridge, with the distance (in either yards or miles) shown on a plate; this may have an arrow to indicate that the bridge is on a side road at a junction ahead.

Older signs not displaying metric and imperial units in one panel will be replaced when they reach the end of their life.

Chord markings used indicate the points between which different headrooms over different parts of an arch bridge are available.

The maximum safe headroom at an arch bridge is shown on the triangular warning signs. Road markings guide high vehicles through the highest part of the arch. Drivers of all vehicles should give way to oncoming high vehicles in the middle of the road when there is insufficient room to pass. Drivers of cars and other low vehicles may keep to the left-hand side of the road, crossing the road markings, where this would enable them to pass oncoming vehicles in safety.

To make a bridge more conspicuous, black and yellow bands may be added to the arches or beams and to the abutments.

Where reduced headroom over a road is due to an overhanging building or structure, a plate may be added below the warning triangle to indicate this ('building' may be varied to 'buildings' or 'structure').

Location of a low bridge
ahead, with indication of
an alternative route

Signs incorporating height restriction roundels and warning triangles

Roundels or warning triangles will
sometimes be incorporated into
directional signs that may also
indicate an alternative route to
take to avoid the low bridge.

Roundels may also be incorporated into road works signs to indicate temporary height restrictions.

Sign indicating a reduction in headroom

Temporary or permanent reduction in bridge headroom ahead (temporary sign)

Level crossing signs and signals

Before the crossing

Level crossing with a gate or barrier

Plate used with level crossing warning signs: advance warning of light signals at a level crossing with or without a gate or barrier

Electrified overhead cable and the safe height beneath it (usually associated with an overhead electrified railway or tramway). On the approach to a junction, the plate may include an arrow to indicate the direction of the level crossing

Level crossing without a gate or barrier

Bells suspended over the road at a railway crossing to give an audible warning to drivers of vehicles that exceed the safe height beneath electrified overhead cables

Drivers of LARGE or SLOW VEHICLES must phone and get permission to cross

LARGE means over 61'6" (18.75 m) long or 9'6" (2.9 m) wide or 44 tonnes total weight SLOW means 5 mph or less

At automatic level crossings, drivers of large or slow vehicles must phone before and after crossing

Long low vehicles may be at risk of grounding; drivers of such vehicles must phone before crossing

Countdown markers may be provided on the approach to a crossing. These divide the distance between the advance warning sign and the stop line into three equal parts; each sloping bar does not necessarily represent a distance of 100 yards

New method of controlling traffic at a crossing ahead (temporary sign)

At the crossing

Some crossings have flashing red road traffic signals; these mean **STOP** (and this applies to pedestrians too). A steady amber light shows before the red lights begin to flash, as at ordinary road traffic signals; this means **STOP** unless it is unsafe to do so. If the red lights flash for more than three minutes without a train arriving (other than at crossings with full barriers), or any barrier is lowered without the lights flashing, phone the signal operator. When the barriers rise, do not proceed until the signals go out. If your vehicle breaks down or stalls on a crossing, get yourself and your passengers out of the vehicle as soon as possible. Phone the signal operator and follow the instructions given. Stand well clear of the crossing if the alarm sounds, the signals show or the barriers lower.

Road traffic signals at a level crossing

Direction to phone

Location of phone

Flashing pedestrian signals used at some level crossings indicate that it is not safe to cross: pedestrians should stop at the pedestrian stop line

EMSWORTH CROSSING

TO CONTACT RAILWAY phone **020 8123 4567**

Name of level crossing and phone number for contacting the railway operator (at level crossings without a dedicated phone)

Yellow box markings indicate an area of carriageway at a level crossing that must be kept clear. Do not enter the box if other stationary traffic may cause you to stop with any part of your vehicle within the box

PARK HERE AND USE PHONE AT CROSSING

Place where drivers of large or slow vehicles should park near a level crossing while contacting the signal operator

Automatic half-barrier level crossings

Amber lights and audible warnings followed by flashing red lights warn that a train is approaching and that the barriers are about to come down. You must **STOP**. The red lights flash all the time the barriers are down, but the audible warning might stop. If another train is approaching, the barriers will stay down; the lights will continue to flash and, if there is an audible warning, the sound will change.

Level crossings with miniature warning lights

These level crossings have gates or barriers but no attendant. The miniature red and green lights are operated by an approaching train. Full directions for using these crossings are given on roadside signs. You must stop even if the gates or barriers have been left open. Always close the gates or barriers after crossing.

Open level crossings

The St Andrew's cross is used at level crossings where there are no gates or barriers. At automatic crossings, **you must always STOP when the traffic light signals show**. At crossings with 'give way' signs, **always look out for and give way to trains.**

Automatic open level crossings have flashing signals and audible warnings. The lights will flash and the warnings will sound until it is safe to cross

If there is more than one railway line over an automatic crossing, this signal will also flash and the sound of the audible warning will change if another train is approaching

Open level crossings without gates, barriers or road traffic light signals have 'give way' signs over a symbol of a railway locomotive

Tram signs, signals and road markings

Trams can run on roads used by other vehicles and pedestrians. The part of the road used by trams (the 'swept path') may have a different colour or textured surface to the rest of the road, or it may be edged with special road markings. **Keep the 'swept path' clear.** Trams cannot move out of the way of other road users!

Route for trams only. The sign may include the bus symbol, the pedal cycle symbol and/or the word 'taxi' where these vehicles may use the tram route

No entry except trams (likely to be used where the route is physically unsuitable for other vehicles)

Indication of a tram-only route at a junction ahead

Warning of trams crossing the road ahead

Reminder to pedestrians to look out for trams approaching from both directions

Drivers of other vehicles must give way to trams at level crossings without barriers, gates or road traffic light signals. Sometimes just a 'give way' sign and a tram plate may be used

Road marking indicating the start of a route for trams only

Alternative road markings indicating the edge of that part of the road used by trams (the swept path)

Examples of signs, signals and road markings for tram drivers

The signal mounted to the right gives instructions to tram drivers; these instructions may not be the same as those given to drivers of other vehicles

Stop unless it is unsafe to do so

Stop

Proceed ahead

Proceed left

Proceed right

Stop line for trams at traffic signals where that part of the road is not used by other vehicles

Speed limit sign for tram drivers shown in kilometres per hour. All diamond-shaped signs are for tram drivers only

Bus and cycle signs and road markings

No vehicles designed to carry more than 8 passengers (excluding driver) or local buses

With-flow bus lane ahead that can also be used by pedal cycles and taxis. Hours of operation may be shown

With-flow bus and pedal cycle lane sign showing hours of operation. Where no times are shown, the bus lane operates at all times

The word 'local' on the bus symbol means the only buses that may use the lane are those running a local service. Where the word 'local' is not shown, the lane may be used by local buses and by any vehicle designed to carry 10 people or more including the driver. Other vehicles may enter and stop in a bus lane to load and unload unless signs alongside the lane indicate otherwise.

Off-side with-flow bus lane ahead that can also be used by pedal cycles

Near-side with-flow bus lane ahead that can also be used by solo motorcycles, pedal cycles and taxis

Near-side with-flow bus lane ahead that can also be used by authorised vehicles, solo motorcycles, pedal cycles and taxis

Off-side with-flow bus lane that can also be used by pedal cycles

Near-side with-flow bus lane that can also be used by solo motorcycles, pedal cycles and taxis

Near-side with-flow bus lane that can also be used by authorised vehicles, solo motorcycles, pedal cycles and taxis

BUS LANE   **BUS GATE**

Road markings indicating the start of a route for buses and other permitted vehicles shown on upright blue circular signs

Bus lane road marking

Traffic may use both lanes at the end of a bus lane

Route for buses and pedal cycles only (older signs may include an 'Only' plate). Cycles not admitted when cycle symbol not shown

Route for buses, pedal cycles, solo motorcycles and taxis only. The motorcycle symbol and word 'taxi' are omitted where these vehicles are not admitted

> **Mon - Fri**
> **8 am - 6 pm**
> **Saturday**
> **8 am - Noon**

Where the route is reserved for buses and/or other permitted vehicles for part of the day only, this is indicated by a time plate

If a bank holiday falls on a day when the restrictions are in operation, the restrictions apply in the normal way.

Bus lane on road at junction ahead

Where there is a break in a bus lane at a junction, other traffic may use the left-hand lane for turning left only

End of bus lane

Contraflow bus lane (the upward arrows indicate the number of traffic lanes available)

Contraflow bus and pedal cycle lane on road at junction ahead

A bus gate is a short length of bus-only street

Reminder to pedestrians to look out for buses, or buses and pedal cycles, approaching from the right

Parking place for buses only, during times shown (with time limit)

Parking place for buses only (no time limit)

Bus Stop

Stopping place
for buses

Photostop only
10 am - 4 pm

Stopping place for
tourist buses to
allow passengers to
take photographs

Except
buses

Except
cycles

Except
buses and
cycles

Except
local buses

Except
buses, taxis
and cycles

Plates used to indicate
exemptions for buses,
taxis and pedal cycles
from prohibitions such
as turn left ahead and no
left turn. These signs are
circular when mounted
in combination with
traffic signals

BUS STAND
No stopping
7 am - 7 pm
except
local buses

Place where local
buses may stand,
from which all
other vehicles are
prohibited during
the times shown

No stopping
7 am - 7 pm
except
local buses

Stopping by
vehicles other
than local buses
prohibited during
the times shown

Edge of carriageway

BUS STOP

Bus stop

Edge of carriageway

BUS STOP

Bus stop in a
lay-by

The broad continuous yellow line at the
edge of the carriageway means that other
vehicles are prohibited from stopping

Entrance to a
bus station,
depot or garage

Mandatory with-flow pedal cycle lane ahead. Hours of operation may be shown

Mandatory with-flow pedal cycle lane. Hours of operation may be shown. Vehicles must not be driven or parked in this lane during its times of operation

Route recommended for pedal cycles on the main carriageway of a road. This may be marked as an advisory pedal cycle lane

Mandatory contraflow pedal cycle lane (the upward arrows indicate the number of traffic lanes available)

Road markings for a mandatory pedal cycle lane

Road markings for an advisory pedal cycle lane. Other vehicles should not use this part of the carriageway unless it is unavoidable

Contraflow pedal cycles in a one-way street (other than a mandatory contraflow cycle lane). This may be marked by a broken line on the carriageway or there may be no line at all

Pedal cycle lane on road at junction ahead or (where 'lane' is varied to 'track') cycle track crossing road at junction ahead

Reminder to pedestrians to look out for pedal cycles approaching from the right

End of cycle lane, track or route

Road marking indicating the end of a cycle lane, track or route

Shared route for pedal cycles and pedestrians only

Separated track and path for pedal cycles and pedestrians

Route for pedal cycles only

Shared route for horses, pedestrians and pedal cycles only

Road marking separating cyclists and pedestrians on a shared route (may be a raised line up to 20 mm high)

Parking place for pedal cycles

No through road except for pedal cycles

Riding of pedal cycles prohibited

Pedal cyclists to rejoin main carriageway at the end of or break in a cycle track or route shared with pedestrians

No entry for vehicular traffic except pedal cycles

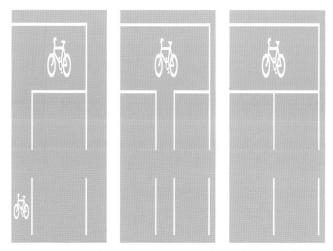

Advance stop line for pedal cycles at traffic signals. When the signals are red, drivers of other vehicles must wait behind the first stop line. Drivers should allow time and space for cyclists to move off when the signals change to green. Cyclists are permitted to cross any part of the first stop line. A cycle lane might not be provided on the approach to the stop line

Pedestrian zone signs

Areas such as shopping streets and streets near/outside schools may be signed as 'pedestrian zones'. Depending on the extent of the vehicle entry restrictions, such areas may be paved without the usual separation between footway and carriageway and may not have yellow lines and kerb markings to indicate waiting and loading restrictions. Instead restrictions are detailed on zone entry signs and repeater plates. The entry signs may indicate that buses, taxis, disabled badge holders or permit holders may enter the zone. There are two types of entry sign depending on whether pedal cycles may be ridden within the zone. Various examples of zone entry signs are shown below.

The yellow panels indicate that there are waiting restrictions within the zone

Signs without yellow panels are used where access may be more restrictive and where waiting restrictions, if any, are indicated by yellow lines within the zone

All vehicles, including ridden pedal cycles, prohibited. (The hours during which a part-time zone operates will be shown in this panel and exemptions in a lower panel)

Ridden pedal cycles permitted within the zone. (The hours during which a part-time zone operates will be shown in this panel and exemptions in a lower panel)

Where different entry restrictions apply at different times of the day, and these restrictions are too complicated to show on the zone entry sign, a sign that can change its display (a variable message sign) may be used. It is therefore important always to check the restrictions in force before entering the zone.

Example of a variable message zone entry sign showing alternative displays for the middle panel (exemptions)

Two examples of waiting restriction repeater signs within the zone. (There may be no yellow lines or kerb markings)

At the end of the zone, a 'zone ends' sign will be displayed. The prohibitory roundel in the upper panel will be a grey version of the roundel shown on the entry sign

On-street parking control signs and road markings

Waiting restrictions

Waiting prohibited 24 hours a day, 7 days a week, throughout the year. Yellow plates are no longer used where the restriction applies all year round

Waiting prohibited between times shown on the sign

Waiting restrictions are indicated by signs and road markings. The restrictions usually apply to the whole of the highway, including verges and footways. Drivers may stop to pick up or set down passengers and, where not prohibited, to load and unload. Disabled badge holders can usually park for up to 3 hours or, in Scotland, without a time limit (see *The Blue Badge Scheme: Rights and Responsibilities in England* published by the Department for Transport, visit www.gov.uk; and *Rights and Responsibilities of a Blue Badge Holder in Scotland* published by Transport Scotland, visit www.mygov.scot).

Yellow lines along the edge of the carriageway, parallel to the kerb, indicate that restrictions are in force. In environmentally sensitive areas, a pale shade of yellow may be used and the width of the lines may be reduced. Except in controlled parking zones (see page 61), small yellow plates are normally erected adjacent to the carriageway to give details of the times of operation of the restrictions. Where the yellow plate does not indicate the days of the week, the restrictions apply at the same times every day, including Sunday. If a bank holiday falls on a day when the restrictions are in operation, the restrictions apply in the normal way unless the plate states that they do not. Special restrictions may apply on days when a large event is being held at a nearby stadium or arena; these will also be shown on the plates.

A double yellow line means no waiting at any time throughout the year. There is normally no vertical yellow plate, except where an older double line remains that applies for only part of the year. The transverse marks at the end of the yellow lines may or may not be provided.

This 'no waiting' sign is used on portable signs to mark temporary waiting restrictions

Length of road to be kept clear of stationary vehicles, at entrances to off-street premises or where the kerb is dropped to provide a convenient crossing place for pedestrians

Loading restrictions

Where loading restrictions apply in addition to waiting restrictions ('loading' means both loading and unloading), these are indicated by yellow kerb marks and white plates. These plates may be combined with the yellow 'no waiting' plates. As the marks are placed intermittently along the kerb, a white plate is normally erected at the first mark (where the loading restriction begins) and may include an arrow indicating the direction along the road in which the loading restriction applies. Where a white plate does not indicate the days of the week, the restrictions apply at the same times every day, including Sunday. If a bank holiday falls on a day when the restrictions are in operation, the restrictions apply in the normal way unless the plate states that they do not.

Loading prohibited
between times
shown on the sign

Special restrictions may apply on days
when a large event is being held at a
nearby stadium or arena; these will also
be shown on the plates. Disabled badge
holders may not park when loading
restrictions are in force.

No loading at any
time throughout
the year

A double kerb mark means no loading
at any time and is normally supplemented
by a 'No loading at any time' plate.
A single kerb mark means that loading
is prohibited during the times shown on
the associated plate.

Examples of waiting and loading restriction signs and markings

No waiting at any time during the summer months in the direction of the
arrow. No waiting at any time throughout the year in the opposite direction
(no yellow plate required). The changeover point is indicated in the
carriageway by the transverse mark on the double yellow lines

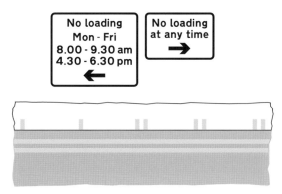

No waiting at any time throughout the year in both directions. No loading to the left during the days and times shown. No loading at any time throughout the year in the opposite direction. The white plates with arrows are placed at the changeover point. There is no transverse mark on the double yellow line because the waiting restrictions do not change

Where two signs are side by side, they may be separate as shown above, combined as shown below or placed in a rectangular arrangement.

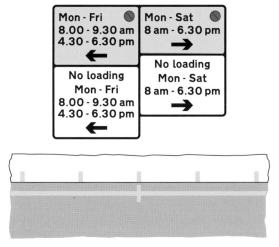

No waiting and loading to the left during morning and evening peak hours on the days shown. No waiting and loading to the right from morning to evening on the days shown. The changeover point for the waiting restrictions is shown by the transverse mark on the single yellow line. The times shown for peak periods and daytime restrictions may vary

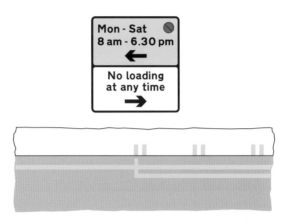

No waiting to the left during the days and times indicated. Loading is permitted at all times in this direction. Waiting and loading prohibited to the right at all times throughout the year. As the double kerb mark has only one meaning, the bottom white panel may be omitted

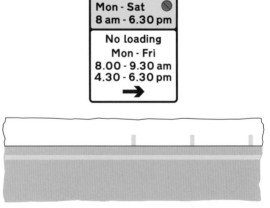

The prohibition of waiting shown on the upper yellow panel on the plate applies in both directions. The prohibition of loading shown on the lower white panel of the plate applies only in the direction of the arrow. In the other direction, loading is permitted at all times. The arrow applies only to the white panel on which it is placed, not to the whole plate. There is no transverse mark on the single yellow line because the waiting restrictions do not change

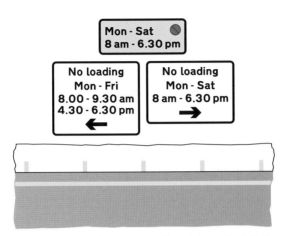

The prohibition of waiting shown on the yellow plate applies in both directions. No loading to the left during morning and evening peak hours on the days shown. No loading to the right from morning to evening on the days shown. The white plates with arrows are placed at the changeover point. There is no transverse mark on the single yellow line because the waiting restrictions do not change. The times shown for peak periods and daytime restrictions may vary

Where there are two or more signs, these may be separate as shown above, combined as shown below or placed in a rectangular arrangement.

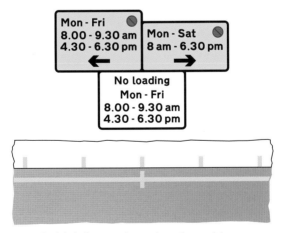

No waiting to the left during morning and evening peak hours.
No waiting to the right from morning to evening on the days shown.
No loading during morning and evening peak hours in both directions.
The changeover point for the waiting restrictions is shown by the transverse mark on the single yellow line

On-street parking places

On-street parking places may be designated for a particular class of vehicle (e.g. solo motorcycles) or for a particular user (e.g. permit holders or disabled badge holders). Parking may be free or paid for (e.g. 'pay and display' or 'pay by phone' or parking meters). There may be a time limit on the period of stay and a minimum time before returning to a particular parking place. Some bays may be designated for use by more than one class of vehicle or user, either at the same time or at different times during the day.

Bays are generally marked in white and are either continuous or divided into individual spaces. A bay may also be indicated by block paving or a change in surfacing colour instead of white lines. Bays may include adjacent words indicating the use of the bay (e.g. 'DISABLED'). The marks and gaps forming the boundary may be any length and may be a continuous line. The double line at the end of a bay with individual spaces is being phased out and replaced by a single broken or continuous white line.

Upright signs are normally erected adjacent to the carriageway to give details of the parking controls. Where a sign does not indicate the days of the week, the restrictions apply at the same times on every day, including Sunday. Where the time of day is not shown, the controls apply for 24 hours. If a bank holiday falls on a day when the controls are in operation, the controls apply in the normal way unless the sign states that they do not. Special controls may apply on days when a large event is being held at a nearby stadium or arena; these will also be shown on the signs. An upright sign may be omitted when a bay marking indicates a single restriction operating at all times.

Edge of carriageway

Parking bay with individual spaces (parallel to the kerb)

Edge of carriageway

Parking bay with individual spaces (echelon)

Edge of carriageway

Continuous parking bay adjacent to the kerb (words may be added outside the bay to describe the type of parking)

Continuous parking bay in the centre of the carriageway (the words are omitted where there is no restriction on the type of user)

Solo motorcycles

Motor cars

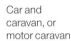

Car and caravan, or motor caravan

Goods vehicles

The above signs indicate free on-street parking places reserved at all times, with no time limit, for particular classes of vehicles. Other signs may indicate more specific parking controls

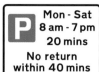

Free parking for all vehicles from Monday to Saturday between 8 am and 7 pm, with a 20-minute time limit (no limit outside those times)

Free parking for motor cars only, from Monday to Saturday between 8 am and 7 pm, with a 20-minute time limit

Free parking for solo motorcycles only, with a one-hour limit at all times

Parking for disabled badge holders only, at all times.

Parking for a specific disabled badge holder with permit 'D123'

Parking for disabled badge holders only, at all times. Outside the hours shown (Monday to Friday), disabled badge holders only may park with no time limit

Parking for permit holders only, at all times

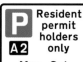

Parking for holders of permit 'A2' only, from Monday to Saturday between 8 am and 6 pm

On-street pay and display parking (the arrow points towards the ticket machine). Days of the week and time periods may be added to indicate when parking must be paid for

Location of ticket
machine for on-street
pay and display
parking

Reminder to
pay and display
at on-street
parking place

Pre-paid voucher parking
only, from Monday to
Saturday between 9 am
and 6 pm, with a two-hour
time limit (lower panel may
give details of voucher)

On-street pay and
display parking where
payment must be
made at a machine

On-street parking
where payment may
be made by phone or
at a machine

On-street parking
where payment may
be made by phone,
text or at a machine

On-street parking
where payment must
be made by phone

On-street pay and
display parking where
first hour is free

Parking for car
club permit holders
'AK-7' only

Electric vehicle recharging point only
Mon - Sat
8 am - 6 pm

Parking for electric vehicle recharging only during times shown (sign may indicate permit holders only)

e-taxi recharging point only
1 hour
No return within 2 hrs

Parking for electric taxi recharging only

Electric solo motorcycle recharging point only

Parking for electric solo motorcycle recharging only (sign may indicate permit holders only)

ASHKEE COUNCIL	
Parking Suspension	
No Loading	
From	14 JULY
Until	21 JULY
Location	500 – 523 PARK ROAD
Purpose	TREE CUTTING

Temporary sign suspending a parking or loading bay to enable works to be carried out

Some residential streets, particularly culs-de-sac, which are reserved for permit holder parking only may not have any signs or bay markings within them, except possibly for a few repeater plates. A sign at the entrance to the street will indicate that parking is for permit holders only.

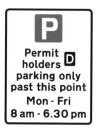

Parking for permit holders only in the street or streets beyond this sign, during the times shown

Resident permit holders parking only in Penfield Close

Except in signed bays

Parking for permit holders only in named street, except where parking bays have been provided for other users.
The lower panel may include the disabled badge holder symbol or the loading symbol

Parking past this point Mon - Fri 9 am - 5 pm

Permit holders AK or 1 hour No return within 1 hour

The parking controls in the street or streets beyond this sign apply from Monday to Friday between 9 am and 5 pm. During these times, permit holders may park with no time limit and other vehicles may park with a one-hour time limit

Parking past this point

8 am - 6 pm Permit holders AK or 2 hours No return within 2 hours

6 pm - 8 am Permit holders AK only

The parking controls in the street or streets beyond this sign apply at all times. During 8 am to 6 pm, permit holders may park with no time limit and other vehicles may park with a two-hour time limit. During 6 pm to 8 am, permit holders only may park

Permit parking area ENDS

End of permit parking area

Where parking-place controls do not operate at all times, any vehicle may park in the bay without payment or time limit unless other restrictions are indicated on the signs.

The upper panel indicates that waiting is prohibited during the morning and evening peak hours (a single yellow line will run through the bay). The lower panel indicates time-limited parking on Monday to Saturday between 10 am and 4 pm. Between 6 pm and 8 am the next day, and all day Sunday, there are no restrictions on parking

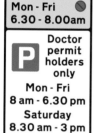

This sign indicates a parking place provided for doctors during the daytime, with a prohibition of waiting between 6.30 am and 8 am (a single yellow line will run through the bay). These restrictions apply from Monday to Friday, with the bay also reserved for doctors on Saturday between 8.30 am and 3 pm

The top panel indicates that waiting is prohibited during the morning and evening peak hours (a single yellow line will run through the bay). The middle panel indicates that loading and unloading are also prohibited during the peak hours (there will be yellow kerb marks alongside the bay). The bottom panel indicates that the bay is used for pay and display parking on Monday to Saturday between 9.30 am and 4.30 pm. Between 6.30 pm and 7.30 am the next day, and all day Sunday, there are no restrictions on parking or loading

Parking bays may be reserved for more than one type of user –
at the same time, at different times, or a combination of both.

P Mon - Sat
7 - 8 am   **Permit holders** Ⓐ   **only**
8 am - 7 pm   **Permit holders** Ⓐ   **or**   **20 mins**   **No return**   **within 40 mins**
7 - 9 pm   **Permit holders** Ⓐ   **only**

The top panel indicates that the parking
controls apply from Monday to Saturday.
Between 7 am and 8 am, and between
7 pm and 9 pm, the parking bay may be
used only by permit holders. Between
8 am and 7 pm, the bay may be used by
permit holders with no time limit, or by any
other vehicle with a 20-minute time limit.
At all other times and on Sunday, the bay
may be used by any vehicle without any
time limit

P
Mon - Sat   **7.30 am - 6.30 pm**
Permit holders Ⓐ   **or**   **20 mins**   **No return**   **within 40 mins**

The parking controls apply from Monday to
Saturday between 7.30 am and 6.30 pm.
During these times the bay may be used by
permit holders, with no time limit, or by any
other vehicle with a 20-minute time limit

P **Mon - Sat**   **10 am - 4 pm**
Permit holders Ⓐ   **or**   **20 mins**   **No return**   **within 40 mins**
At other times   **and Sunday**   **Permit holders** Ⓐ   **only**

The parking bay is reserved for permit
holders, without time limit, at all times.
Other vehicles may also use the bay, but
only from Monday to Saturday between
10 am and 4 pm, with a 20-minute time limit

Parking on verge and footway

Although vehicles should not be parked on verges and footways (it is unlawful in London, in some other cities and generally throughout Scotland), this may be allowed on certain narrow streets where parked vehicles would not obstruct pedestrians. There are special signs to indicate footway parking. There may also be white bays indicating where parking is permitted. Where there are controls applying to the parking place, such as pay and display, these should be indicated by separate signs.

Vehicles may be parked partially on the verge or footway

Vehicles may be parked wholly on the verge or footway

Vehicles may be parked partially on the verge or footway during the times shown

End of verge or footway parking

Vehicles may be parked partially on the footway in marked bays only

Vehicles may be parked partially on the verge or footway, with a one-hour time limit

Entrance to an area where parking on the verge or footway is prohibited

Reminder to drivers that parking on the verge or footway is prohibited

End of an area where parking on the verge or footway is prohibited

Loading bays and loading areas

Special loading bays may be provided along with parking bays, or in areas where waiting and loading are otherwise prohibited. The bays may be reserved for use by goods vehicles (where indicated on signs) or may be used by all vehicles, e.g. outside shops where heavy purchases have to be carried to a car. However, these bays should not be used prior to making the purchase, but only for collection of pre-paid items when they are too large or heavy to carry to where the car is parked. Once loading is complete, the vehicle must leave the bay. Some loading bays may be used for other purposes at different times of the day. For example, the bay may be reserved for disabled badge holders during the day and for loading during early morning and late afternoon. In such cases the bay will **not** be marked 'LOADING ONLY'; it is therefore important to read the upright signs to see who can use the bay at certain times of day. There may be times, such as morning and evening peak periods, when loading is not permitted. In such cases, there will be a single yellow line running through the bay and single 'no loading' marks on the kerb. The length of the white marks and gaps forming the boundary of a loading bay no longer have fixed sizes. The boundary may be formed by a continuous white line. A loading bay may also be indicated by coloured surfacing or block paving instead of white lines.

Bay reserved for loading and unloading by all vehicles at all times

Edge of carriageway

Loading bay (conditions of use shown on upright sign)

Goods vehicles loading only Mon - Sat 10 am - 4 pm

Bay reserved for loading and unloading by goods vehicles only during the times shown

Mon - Sat 7 - 10 am 4 - 6 pm

No loading Mon - Sat 7 - 10 am 4 - 6 pm

Loading only 10 am - 4 pm

Waiting and loading are prohibited from Monday to Saturday during the times shown in the top and middle panels. The bay may be used for loading only during the times shown in the bottom panel, including Sunday

Loading only past this point Mon - Sat 8 am - 6 pm

Entrance to a loading-only area where no other type of parking is permitted during the times shown

7.30 - 9.00 am Loading only

9 am - 4.30 pm Disabled badge holders only

4.30 - 7.00 pm Loading only

Parking place with different uses at different times of day. The parking controls apply every day between 7.30 am and 7 pm. Between 7.30 am and 9 am, and between 4.30 pm and 7 pm, the bay may be used for loading and unloading only with no time limit. Between 9 am and 4.30 pm, the bay may be used by disabled badge holders only. At all other times not shown on the sign, the bay may be used by any user without any time limit

Off-highway areas may be designated 'loading areas' where waiting is restricted except by permitted vehicles. Signs are used without road markings to indicate this.

Entrance to a loading area

Repeater sign within a loading area

End of loading area

Controlled parking zones

Entrance to a controlled parking zone

End of controlled or voucher parking zone

Some areas are designated as controlled parking zones. The entry sign indicates the times when waiting is prohibited. The yellow lines within the zone **do not normally have yellow plates** indicating the times of the prohibition unless the times are different from those shown on the entry sign. It is therefore important to note the times shown when entering the zone. If there is no lower panel showing days and times, the zone operates at all times. If loading is prohibited at the same time as the waiting prohibition, the entry sign should include the words 'No loading' at the bottom of the upper panel. The zone is likely to include parking places and loading bays. Some parking places may be for permit holders only, others for general use. The times when these operate should be shown on the signs at the bays; these times may not be the same as those shown on the zone entry sign. Where the majority of on-street parking within the zone is pay and display, the heading on the entry sign may say 'Pay and Display ZONE' instead of 'Controlled ZONE'.

Other headings might be 'Meter ZONE' where there are parking meters, or 'Disc ZONE' where a parking disc showing the time of arrival has to be displayed on the vehicle when parking. The entry sign to a pre-paid voucher parking zone includes the voucher logo.

Sign at a parking bay within a disc zone. Free parking for all vehicles, with a 30-minute time limit from Monday to Saturday between 8 am and 6 pm. A parking disc indicating the time of arrival at the parking bay must be displayed in the vehicle

Entrance to a voucher parking zone

In some areas, local authorities operate special goods vehicle waiting restrictions. Usually these apply to goods vehicles of over 5 or 7.5 tonnes maximum gross weight. Where the same restrictions apply throughout a zone, usually overnight, the times are indicated on a zone entry sign. Within the zone there are no yellow lines (unless there are other waiting restrictions applying to all vehicles), but there should be repeater signs on each side of every street as a reminder. There are equivalent signs for buses with the bus symbol, and signs that apply to both goods vehicles and buses.

Zone entry

Repeater sign indicating the times when waiting by goods vehicles over the maximum gross weight shown is prohibited

Zone exit

Restricted parking zones

In some environmentally sensitive areas, where waiting and loading restrictions are uniform, they may be indicated by upright repeater signs, but not yellow lines and kerb marks. These are known as restricted parking zones. The zone entry sign indicates the times when waiting and loading are prohibited. Where parking and loading are permitted, usually in signed bays, this should be indicated on the entry signs. The bays within the zone may be fully marked in the conventional manner or indicated by other means such as a change in surface materials. Upright signs will give details about the use of the bays.

Entrance to a restricted parking zone where both waiting and loading are prohibited during the times shown in the lower panel. The words 'No loading' are omitted where loading is not prohibited

Entrance to a restricted parking zone where both waiting and loading are prohibited during the times shown in the lower panel. The words 'No loading' are omitted where loading is not prohibited

Repeater sign within a restricted parking zone. The lower panel is omitted where loading is not prohibited

End of restricted parking zone

63

Provision may be made for parking and loading within a zone, with bays being delineated either by white road markings or by physical features, such as block paving, planters or bollards. As well as normal parking bay signs, these examples may be seen where the operational times are different from those of the whole zone.

Clearways

 The red cross means no stopping, not even to pick up or set down passengers. The sign is used to indicate a 24-hour clearway (usually on a rural road) or may be incorporated into other signs with the words 'No stopping' (e.g. the 'no stopping except local buses' sign at bus stops). On a 24-hour clearway, the prohibition of stopping applies to the main running carriageway, slip roads and any acceleration and deceleration areas. You may stop in a lay-by unless there are signs to say otherwise. A 24-hour clearway does not have any special road markings, but smaller repeater signs might be provided at intervals along the road as a reminder to drivers.

Start of 24-hour clearway (no stopping on main carriageway at any time for the distance shown)

End of 24-hour clearway

This sign is used on a 24-hour clearway where waiting is prohibited on the verge or footway in addition to the prohibition of stopping on the main carriageway. The words 'on verge or footway' may be varied to 'on verge' or 'on footway'. Where the 'no waiting' symbol is replaced by the red cross, stopping on the verge or footway is prohibited

In built-up areas, urban clearways may be provided. During the times the urban clearway is in operation, stopping is not allowed on the carriageway or verges, except to pick up or set down passengers. There are no special road markings, but the signs are usually repeated throughout the length of the clearway, mainly after each road junction

End of urban clearway

Stopping in lay-by not allowed, except in an emergency (similar to hard shoulders on a motorway). This may not apply to the whole lay-by. The length over which stopping is prohibited will be indicated by double yellow lines. These lay-bys usually have an emergency telephone

Yellow zig-zag markings outside schools, hospitals or fire, police or ambulance stations indicate the length of road where you should not stop, not even to pick up or set down children or other passengers. Where there is an upright sign, there is a mandatory prohibition of stopping during the times shown. These markings are provided outside schools to ensure that children can see and be seen clearly when crossing the road

Red routes

On red routes, yellow waiting restriction lines are replaced by red lines that mean no stopping for any purpose, not even to pick up or set down passengers, other than by a licensed taxi. A driver of a vehicle displaying a disabled badge may stop to pick up or set down a disabled person, but must not park.

Double red lines mean no stopping at any time (upright signs might not be provided)

Single red lines mean no stopping during the days and times shown on the upright sign

The prohibition of stopping applies to the whole road, including the verge and footway, during the times shown on upright signs that face oncoming traffic. Special bays marked on the carriageway may be provided for parking or loading; the conditions that apply to these will be indicated on upright signs that should also face oncoming traffic.

RED ROUTE

No stopping
Mon - Sat
7 am - 7 pm

Except 10 am - 4 pm

 loading
max 20 mins

 max 3 hours

RED ROUTE

No stopping
Mon - Sat
7 am - 7 pm

Except

 max 3 hours

A bay marked with red lines means that it is available for use for only part of the time that the red route 'no stopping' rule applies. The bay must not be used from Monday to Saturday between 7 am and 10 am nor between 4 pm and 7 pm. In this example, the bay may be used for loading/unloading (maximum stay 20 minutes) and by disabled badge holders (maximum stay 3 hours), during the times shown in the bottom panel

A bay marked with white lines means that it is available for use at all times that the red route 'no stopping' rule applies. The upright sign shown in this example means that the bay is reserved for disabled badge holders only (maximum stay 3 hours) during the times shown in the middle panel. Outside these hours, any user may park there with no limit

Where a taxi rank is provided on a red route, the broad yellow line is replaced by a single or double red line as appropriate. Upright 'red route' signs will indicate the times when stopping is prohibited. Where the bay is used by other vehicles at other times, red route bay markings will be provided.

Licensed taxis may pick up or set down passengers at bus stops on a red route where there is a double red line or a broad continuous yellow line, but not if the broad line is red. Drivers of vehicles displaying a disabled badge are not permitted to stop for any purpose in a bus stop bay where there is either a broad yellow or broad red line. The broad yellow line is to be phased out on red routes and replaced by either a double red line, a single red line or a broad red line as appropriate

Some red routes have upright signs without any road markings. These are designated 'RED ROUTE CLEARWAYS', where stopping for any purpose is prohibited at all times, except in marked lay-bys. Unlike the 24-hour clearway on rural roads, stopping on a red route clearway is prohibited on the verge and footway as well as on the main carriageway. Signs are usually repeated throughout the length of the clearway.

Start of a red route clearway
(also used as a repeater sign,
particularly after a road junction)

End of red route
clearway

Taxi ranks

Taxi ranks usually have yellow bays marked with the word 'TAXIS'. Where the bay is used as a parking or loading bay at a different time of day, a white bay without any words is provided. Either waiting or stopping will be prohibited within a taxi rank. Where stopping is prohibited, the taxi rank includes a broad continuous yellow line at the edge of the carriageway. Yellow 'no waiting' lines are provided within a yellow taxi rank where waiting is also prohibited at other times. Yellow upright signs show the times when waiting or stopping is prohibited in the rank.

No waiting in taxi rank during the times shown

No stopping in taxi rank during the times shown. The bay includes a broad continuous line to indicate the prohibition of stopping

Waiting is prohibited at all times (indicated by double yellow lines). The taxi rank operates from 11 pm to 5 am every day

The taxi rank operates every day between 10 am and 4 pm. Waiting is otherwise prohibited from 8 am to 6 pm every day, and loading is prohibited during the morning and evening peak hours from Monday to Friday

The taxi rank operates overnight (11 pm to 5 am) on each day of the week, during which time waiting by other vehicles is prohibited. The rank is used as a goods vehicle loading bay between 10 am and 4 pm from Monday to Saturday. There are no restrictions on parking during the times when the bay is not being used as a taxi rank or a goods vehicle loading bay. Where the single yellow line does not extend beyond the end the bay (as shown), it might not have transverse marks at each end

The taxi rank operates overnight (11 pm to 5 am) on each day of the week, during which time stopping by other vehicles is prohibited. The rank is used as a parking bay between 9 am and 6 pm with waiting limited to 20 minutes. There are no restrictions on parking outside these times

Information boards may be provided at taxi ranks

E-taxi ranks

At locations where taxi ranks are reserved for the sole use of electric taxis, bays are marked with the legend 'E-TAXIS' and a yellow upright sign.

No stopping in e-taxi rank at any time. The bay includes a broad continuous line to indicate the prohibition of stopping

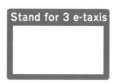

Information boards may be provided at e-taxi ranks

73

Road markings

Along the road

Centre line on a single carriageway road

Lane line separating traffic travelling in the same direction (single or dual carriageway road)

Hazard warning line (replaces a centre line or a lane line). An upright sign may indicate the nature of the hazard, such as a bend. The marking is used also on the approach to a junction

Diagonal white lines (hatched markings) bounded by broken lines may be used in the centre of the road to separate opposing flows of traffic. They are often provided at junctions to protect traffic turning right. They may also be used on the approach to a central traffic island or the start of a dual carriageway. Hatched markings with a single, broken boundary line may be used at the edge of the road or next to the central reservation of a dual carriageway: the diagonal lines always slope towards the direction of travel. You should not enter any hatched area bounded by a broken line unless it is safe to do so

Part of the carriageway where traffic passes in the same direction on either side of the chevron marking. Vehicles should not enter the area unless it is safe to do so. This marking is likely to be found in one-way streets with central islands and where an exit lane leaves at a junction

Part of the carriageway where traffic passes in the same direction on either side of the chevron marking. The continuous boundary line means that vehicles must not enter the area except in an emergency. This marking is used where slip roads leave and join motorways and many dual carriageway roads. It is also used for segregated left-turn lanes at roundabouts

Reduction in the number of lanes, or area not available to traffic. Vehicles must not cross the continuous white line except in an emergency. Used on the right-hand side of a motorway, dual carriageway road or slip road

Arrow indicating the direction in which to pass hatched markings and double white lines, or the route that high vehicles should take under a low arch bridge (may be reversed)

Double white lines

These are used to prevent overtaking where visibility is restricted, and to separate opposing traffic flows on steep hills with climbing lanes. Double continuous lines are also sometimes used on other single carriageway roads that have two lanes in at least one direction. Viewed in the direction of travel, if the line closest to you is continuous, you must not cross or straddle it (except to turn into or out of a side road or property, avoid a stationary vehicle blocking the lane, or overtake a pedal cycle, horse or road works vehicle moving at not more than 10 mph). Where the line closest to you is broken, you may cross the lines to overtake if it is safe to do so. Stopping is prohibited on any length of road that has double white lines, even if the line on that side of the road is broken. The exceptions are stopping to pick up or set down passengers, or to load or unload. In these circumstances, you should park off the main carriageway wherever possible.

Some double continuous white lines have narrow areas of hatched lines within them or a wider area of hatching to the side. You must not cross a continuous white line to enter a hatched area

Overtaking lanes

A single carriageway road might sometimes have two lanes in one direction to provide an overtaking lane and one lane in the other. The opposing traffic flows are separated by continuous double white lines. This arrangement then changes to provide the overtaking lane in the opposite direction. Upright signs indicate the number of lanes in each direction and the end of the overtaking lane.

Road marking in the centre of the road at the end of an overtaking lane where two lanes reduce to one. You must not cross the continuous white line and enter the hatched area, except for the reasons mentioned for double white lines

Signs on primary routes have green backgrounds with white arrows. Signs on non-primary routes have white backgrounds with black arrows.

Overtaking lane continues for the distance shown, with single lane traffic in the opposite direction. This arrangement may then change to provide the overtaking lane in the opposite direction

End of overtaking lane ahead

Single lane traffic with two lanes in the opposite direction

Along the edge of the road

Side elevation

Edge of carriageway, other than at junctions, exits from private drives and lay-bys. Used on the left-hand side of the road and alongside the central reservation of dual carriageway roads

Alternative edge of carriageway marking, with raised ribs to provide audible and tactile warnings when the line is being crossed. They are used on motorways and other roads with hard shoulders or hard marginal strips

Edge of main carriageway at a junction where a slip road or lane leaves or joins, at an exit from a private drive or at a lay-by. Also used to divide the main carriageway from a traffic lane that leaves the main carriageway at a junction ahead (lane drop)

Edge of main carriageway at a junction or at an exit from a private drive. Used in conjunction with 'give way' markings on the side road

At junctions

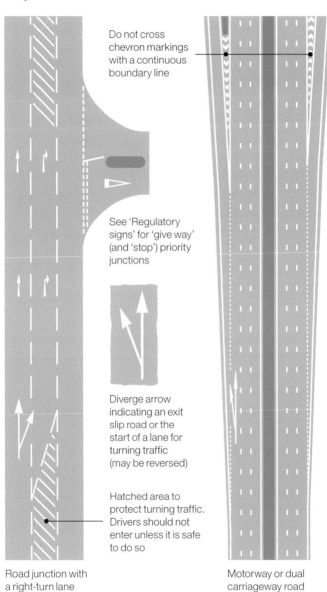

Do not cross chevron markings with a continuous boundary line

See 'Regulatory signs' for 'give way' (and 'stop') priority junctions

Diverge arrow indicating an exit slip road or the start of a lane for turning traffic (may be reversed)

Hatched area to protect turning traffic. Drivers should not enter unless it is safe to do so

Road junction with a right-turn lane

Motorway or dual carriageway road with exit and entry slip roads

79

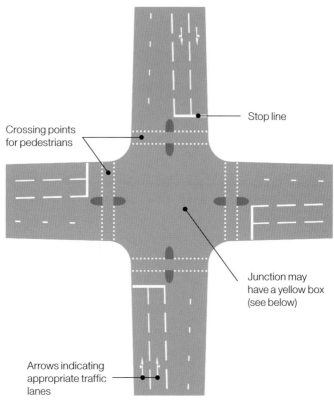

Stop line

Crossing points for pedestrians

Junction may have a yellow box (see below)

Arrows indicating appropriate traffic lanes

Junction with traffic signals

Where stationary traffic would be likely to block a junction, a yellow box may be marked on the road, covering all or part of the junction. You must not enter the box if your exit is not clear. If turning right at the junction, you may enter the box (behind other right-turning vehicles, if any) to wait for a gap in the oncoming traffic, but only if the right-turn exit is clear

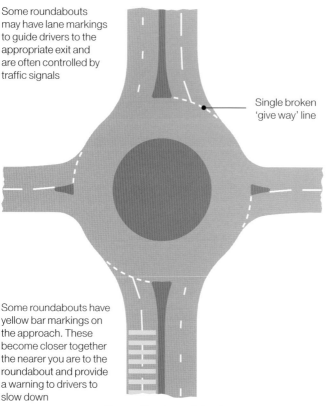

Some roundabouts may have lane markings to guide drivers to the appropriate exit and are often controlled by traffic signals

Single broken 'give way' line

Some roundabouts have yellow bar markings on the approach. These become closer together the nearer you are to the roundabout and provide a warning to drivers to slow down

Conventional roundabout

A mini-roundabout is normally found on a road with a speed limit of 30 mph or less. It should be treated the same as a conventional roundabout. You must give way to traffic from the right, and keep to the left of the white circle unless the size of your vehicle or the junction layout makes driving over it unavoidable

Mini-roundabout

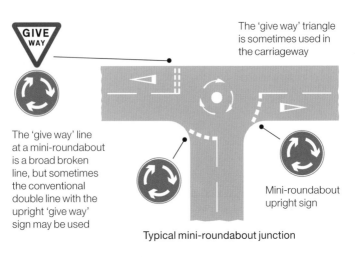

The 'give way' triangle is sometimes used in the carriageway

The 'give way' line at a mini-roundabout is a broad broken line, but sometimes the conventional double line with the upright 'give way' sign may be used

Mini-roundabout upright sign

Typical mini-roundabout junction

Central island of roundabout

Segregated left-turn lane

Longthorpe B 6234

Maverton A 6604

Doncastle A 6604

Some conventional roundabouts may have a segregated left-turn lane where drivers do not give way to traffic on the roundabout. This may be separated from the roundabout by either a solid island or chevron markings. Where the chevrons are bounded by continuous lines, vehicles must not enter the area except in an emergency. You should therefore choose the correct lane well before the roundabout. A directional sign in advance of the junction may show the segregated lane

Traffic lanes at junctions

Appropriate traffic lanes for different movements at junction ahead. A double-headed arrow is used where two different movements may be made from the same lane or where that lane divides into two or more lanes ahead (e.g. a lane with a combined 'left' and 'ahead' arrow may divide into a left-turn lane and an ahead lane)

Compulsory traffic movements at a junction ahead. These may apply to a specific traffic lane or to all traffic approaching the junction

Direction to be taken by traffic turning within a junction

Appropriate traffic lanes for particular destinations

Worded markings

Direction in which pedestrians should look before crossing the road (particularly in a one-way street or where there is a contraflow bus lane)

Area of carriageway to be kept clear of stationary traffic, usually to allow the passage of vehicles into or out of a side road or access. The white bars may be omitted

Vehicles must not pass this marking. May be used with the upright 'no entry' sign

Associated with a hazard. There will normally be an upright warning sign

Road studs

Central reservation

Coloured road studs help drivers at night, especially on wet roads, or in poor visibility. White studs mark traffic lanes or the centre of the road. The left-hand side of the carriageway is marked by red studs, and the edge of the central reservation of a motorway or dual carriageway road by amber studs. Green studs are used to mark lay-bys and the entrances to, and exits from, slip roads.

Traffic calming

Traffic calming is the term used to describe physical features provided along a road to encourage drivers to reduce speed. These features are introduced for the safety of all road users, particularly pedestrians and cyclists. Traffic-calming schemes can employ a variety of measures, including road humps and narrowings. Warning signs often indicate the type of measure to be expected. There may be an entry sign at the boundary of an area that has traffic-calming features.

Entrance to a traffic-calmed area. The name of the area may be shown. The sign may also be used in advance of the area and show a distance. Where the traffic-calmed area is reached by turning into a side road, the sign will include an arrow

Road humps

Road humps may have a flat or round top, extending across the width of the road or covering a whole junction. They may also be in the form of a 'cushion', covering only part of a traffic lane and designed to allow buses and large emergency vehicles to straddle them, while slowing other vehicles. Warning signs may be erected at the beginning of the road where a hump or series of humps is installed.

Road humps for distance shown. May be varied to 'Hump' with distance omitted

Alternative plates used with 'road hump' sign

Humps for 300 yards →

Road humps for distance shown and in direction indicated

Hump 20 yds →

Road hump in the distance and direction indicated

A road hump is normally marked with white triangle and edge line markings.

Zebra, parallel and signal-controlled pedestrian crossings are sometimes located on flat-top humps. These may be indicated by advance warning signs.

Zebra or parallel crossing on a road hump

Signal-controlled pedestrian crossing on a road hump

Road narrowings

Roads may be reduced in width by the use of build-outs on one or both sides. When placed on both sides, they may be opposite each other or staggered. Priority through the narrowing may be controlled by signs and 'give way' markings. It is essential that you obey signs indicating priority to vehicles coming from the opposite direction.

Give way to oncoming vehicles

Priority over oncoming vehicles

If priority is not given to either direction at a road narrowing, you should ensure that you can pass through without endangering occupants in vehicles approaching from the other direction. Do not accelerate on the approach to a narrowing, but maintain a steady low speed and be prepared to give way to approaching traffic. Let any cyclists proceed ahead of you.

Road narrows on left (right if symbol reversed)

Road narrows on both sides

Warning signs indicating which side the narrowing occurs may be used in advance, especially where priority signs and markings are not provided.

20 mph zones

Entrance to a 20 mph zone

End of 20 mph zone and start of 30 mph speed limit

Some traffic-calmed areas are indicated by the 20 mph zone entry sign. This sign, as well as indicating a 20 mph speed limit, warns drivers that they are entering an area with traffic-calming features, such as road humps and road narrowings. These features may not be individually signed and, in these areas, it is important that you adopt a steady low speed and avoid repeated acceleration and deceleration. The zone might include 20 mph speed limit repeater signs and road markings.

Home Zones

Home Zones are residential areas with streets designed to be places for people as well as for motor traffic. The road space is shared among drivers and other road users. People could be using the whole of the space for a range of activities. You should drive slowly and carefully and be prepared to stop to allow people extra time to make room for you to pass them in safety.

Entrance to a
Home Zone

End of
Home Zone

Quiet Lanes

Some minor rural roads in England and Wales may be designated as Quiet Lanes. These are appropriate for shared use by walkers, cyclists, horse riders and motor vehicles. You should drive slowly and carefully and be prepared to stop to allow people extra time to make room for you to pass them in safety.

Start of designated
Quiet Lane

End of
Quiet Lane

Share space

This is a street or place designed to reduce the dominance of motor vehicles and where motorists, cyclists and pedestrians should expect to share the same space. Motorists should drive slowly and carefully and be prepared to stop to allow pedestrians and cyclists extra time to make room to pass them in safety.

Share space road
or place ahead

Other features

Rumble devices across the road, either in the form of strips or larger areas, may be used to provide a visual, audible and vibratory effect, often in rural locations. The intention is to alert drivers to a hazard ahead, usually a bend or road junction, and encourage them to reduce speed. A warning sign may be used in association with a rumble device to identify the hazard, but the device itself is not the hazard and is not usually specifically signed.

Gateways into villages may be formed from the combination of speed limit signs, yellow backing boards and village name plates. Central hatched markings or islands may also be used to separate opposing traffic. Drivers approaching the gateways should reduce speed and observe the speed limit all the way through the village.

Example of a village gateway

Some parts of the carriageway may have a coloured surface to emphasise the road markings.

Motorway signs, signals and road markings

Most motorway signs have a blue background with white lettering, numbers and borders, although tourist destination signs, as on other roads, have brown backgrounds (see page 98).

Start of motorway regulations

Special traffic regulations govern the use of motorways. These include no stopping (except, in an emergency, on the hard shoulder or verge), no U-turns and no reversing. Goods vehicles and buses (where a bus is a vehicle constructed to carry more than eight seated passengers) with a maximum laden weight of more than 7.5 tonnes, vehicles drawing trailers, and vehicles required to be fitted with a speed limiter, must not use the right-hand lane of a motorway that has three or more lanes. Motorways must not be used by certain classes of traffic: invalid carriages of less than 254 kg unladen weight, pedal cycles, motorcycles under 50 cc capacity, agricultural vehicles and vehicles incapable of attaining a speed of 25 mph on the level when unladen and not drawing a trailer. Pedestrians and animals are also prohibited.

To ensure that direction signs are absolutely clear to drivers travelling at motorway speeds, it is necessary to limit the number of destinations shown. Your destination might not appear on the motorway signs: when planning a journey, it is advisable before setting off to check the junction number of the exit you require. Junctions can be identified by the number shown on a black background in the bottom left-hand or top left-hand corner of motorway signs (or, in the case of overhead signs, in a separate panel also indicating the distance to the junction). Junction numbers are usually shown on road maps, so it is easy to check these before starting your journey. On the motorway, these numbers can be used as a guide to your location. However, not all junctions have an exit in both directions, so numbers may not be consecutive. Where new junctions have been constructed, the number may be followed by a letter (e.g. junction 23A).

A road other than a motorway is called an 'all-purpose road'.
At the point where you join a motorway, a special symbol is used
to indicate the start of motorway regulations. A direction sign on
an all-purpose road will normally use this symbol to indicate a
motorway slip road or the beginning of a motorway. Where a sign
shows a motorway route number on a blue background without
the symbol, the route indicated will normally be an all-purpose
road that you should follow to reach the motorway.

Blue direction signs, with the motorway symbol and large route numbers,
indicate that a motorway or motorway slip road leads directly from a
junction with an all-purpose road. The motorway junction number, shown
on the black background, may not always be included

On the approach to a junction with a motorway, a direction sign on an
all-purpose road has blue panels that include the motorway symbol.
The panels may include the junction number on a black background.
The name in capital letters is a regional destination

This sign, with the motorway number
in brackets on a blue background, but
without the motorway symbol,
indicates the route to take from a
junction ahead in order to reach
the motorway. The motorway is not
accessed directly from this junction

Signs for junctions on the motorway

On the approach to a junction, direction signs are usually located 1 mile and ½ mile in advance, and at the exit point. Where junctions are close together, these distances may be reduced, normally to ⅔ mile and ⅓ mile respectively. The signs may be mounted at the side of the road or overhead.

Signs located at the side of the motorway. These are used where there is a deceleration lane. The number of lanes through the junction remains the same

The first two signs on the approach to a junction show the destination and the route number for the exit only. The distance shown (usually 1 mile or ½ mile) is the distance to the exit (start of the deceleration lane). The junction number is shown on the black background

This sign is located at the start of the deceleration lane and includes destinations reached by staying on the motorway

A final route direction sign is usually located where the exit slip road separates from the main carriageway

Countdown markers indicate the distance to the start of the deceleration lane. Each bar represents about 100 yards

Overhead sign for junctions with deceleration lanes, where the number of lanes through the junction remains the same

This sign is used on the approach to the junction (usually 1 mile and ½ mile in advance) and at the start of the deceleration lane. Destinations and route numbers are shown for both the exit and the motorway ahead. Countdown markers are normally provided for the deceleration lane

Signs located at the side of the motorway where one or more lanes leave the main carriageway to become the exit slip road. This type of junction is known as a lane drop

This sign is normally located 1 mile and ½ mile before the junction and shows the appropriate lanes to use for various destinations. In this example, the left-hand lane leads directly to the exit slip road; the centre and right-hand lanes continue through the junction

This sign, with the inclined arrow, is normally located just before the left-hand lane leaves the main carriageway

Overhead signs for a lane-drop junction

This sign is used both in advance and at the junction

A confirmatory sign may be provided just after the point where the slip road has separated from the main carriageway. It is used where signs on the approach to the junction are either overhead or located at the side of the motorway

Lane-drop junctions do not use the countdown markers shown on page 93, as there is no deceleration lane for drivers to move into. A special road marking is used at lane drops (see pages 78 and 95) between the main carriageway and the lane that leads to the exit slip road. This marking usually commences at the ½ mile advance sign.

Some junction layouts may be more complex and designed to allow a heavier flow of traffic to leave the motorway. A traffic lane may be shared by traffic both continuing ahead and leaving the motorway. This shared lane has a deceleration lane separated from a lane drop by chevron road markings. In the example, the left-hand lane is used for the exit slip road only, the centre lane is the shared lane, and the right-hand lane is for ahead traffic only. A sign mounted at the side of the motorway shows the road layout. An overhead sign shows the appropriate lanes to use for each destination.

Central reservation

A sign mounted at the side of the motorway shows the arrangement of traffic lanes

Overhead sign showing appropriate lanes for the different destinations

Other types of sign in advance of junctions

Where the junction ahead is with another motorway, additional signs may be provided prior to the 1 mile advance sign

Where two junctions are very close, they may both be shown on the same sign, together with the distances and junction numbers. The sign that is located where the deceleration lane starts for the first exit (see page 93) will normally show the second exit place names and route number with the ahead destinations

This overhead sign indicates a junction that has two exits. The first exit has a deceleration lane and is indicated by the upper part of the sign. The second exit is a lane drop. Traffic continuing along the motorway should use the centre and right-hand lanes

Signs showing lanes that join the main carriageway at junctions

Sign for drivers on slip road

Sign for drivers on main carriageway

The slip road joins the main carriageway as a lane gain to increase the number of lanes from two to three. A distance panel may be added

Sign for drivers on slip road

Sign for drivers on main carriageway

The right-hand lane of the slip road joins the main carriageway as a merge with an acceleration lane. This is followed by the left-hand lane which joins the main carriageway as a lane gain. Chevron road markings normally separate the two lanes on the slip road. The distance may be omitted

Direction signs on exit slip roads (the green panels indicate a primary route; the white panels indicate a non-primary route)

Directions from junction ahead, usually controlled by traffic signals or a 'give way' sign

Directions from a roundabout ahead

Motorway-to-motorway junction with a roundabout (motorway regulations continue to apply)

Appropriate lanes to use on the approach to the junction (sign located at the side of the slip road)

Appropriate lanes to use on the approach to the junction (overhead sign over the slip road)

Appropriate lanes for turning movements at junction ahead

Direction signs where the main carriageway of a motorway ends at a roundabout

Motorway ends at a junction with an all-purpose road

Motorway ends at a junction with another motorway

Signs for tourist destinations

Tourist destinations are shown on signs with brown backgrounds. On the main carriageway of a motorway, these are separate from the main direction signs and are usually sited ¾ mile and ¼ mile from the junction (although they do not show the distance to the junction). On exit slip roads and where the motorway ends at a roundabout, the main direction signs may show tourist destinations on a brown panel, in the same way that they show other destinations on green and white panels (see page 97). However, separate brown signs are likely to be used at these locations to avoid putting too much information on a single sign. See pages 118 to 120 for more information about tourist signs.

Sign at the side of the main carriageway. There will usually be two of these in advance of the junction

Sign indicating a place with several tourist attractions. It is located at the side of the main carriageway on the approach to a junction

Sign on exit slip road indicating directions to tourist attractions from a roundabout ahead

Sign on exit slip road indicating directions to tourist attractions from a junction ahead

Where it is not practicable to provide tourist destination signs within 1 mile of a junction or there are more destinations than can be accommodated on the signs, this sign may be used in advance of the main 1 mile direction sign for the junction. It may also be used when the junction layout is complex (such as that shown on page 95); 'leave at Junction 24' is then varied to 'follow' plus a destination

Signs for motorway service areas

On most motorways, service areas are provided at intervals of not more than 30 miles, half an hour at normal motorway driving speeds. These service areas are open 24 hours a day, every day of the year, and provide fuel, free parking (up to 2 hours), refreshments, toilets and disabled access. Other facilities, including telephones, motels and tourist information, may also be provided. Some motorway service areas are accessed directly from the main carriageway, others via junctions with other roads, where they will also be available to non-motorway traffic.

Services
10 m

After each junction, a sign may show the distance to the next motorway service area

Services	
M 4	16 m
M 5 (N)	22 m
M 5 (S)	27 m

This sign may be used when there is a junction with another motorway before the next service area

Services		
M 4	STEAKADE	1 m
	ROADCOOK	20 m
M 5 (N)	WOODHOUSE FIFTY	10 m
M 5 (S)	NO SERVICES	

About 1 mile in advance of a service area, a sign may inform drivers of the availability of services ahead, including the names of the operators. It will normally show the next two services, and include services on other motorways if the junctions with those motorways are reached before the second service area. Where the first services are located at a junction, this sign is likely to be used about 2 miles in advance; the word 'Services' may be added to the junction direction

About ½ mile before the service area (further if the services are at a junction), a sign informs drivers of the facilities available, and may include both the name of the operator and the geographical name. The price of fuel, if shown, is usually for a litre of unleaded petrol, indicated by the green pump symbol. The 'vehicle and plug' symbol means that facilities for recharging electric vehicles are available; the 'i' symbol refers to an information point; the bed symbol indicates overnight accommodation

Sign located at start of the deceleration lane for a service area with direct access from the motorway

99

Motorway service area signs may display placeholders that contain the corporate identifier of a franchise operating on the site

Sign indicating a motorway truckstop where parking, refreshments, toilets and fuel are available 24 hours a day throughout the year

Alternative signs indicating the entrance to a service area accessed directly from a motorway. May be used to indicate the direction to a motorway service area located on an all-purpose road

Where a motorway service area is situated on an all-purpose road, the sign off the motorway indicating the services should have a blue background. The geographical name of the services may be shown on this sign. The word 'Services' may be incorporated into other direction signs, including the sign on the exit slip road from the motorway.

Motorway service area ahead on an all-purpose road (sign located off the motorway)

Direction or entrance to a motorway service area located on an all-purpose road (alternative signs)

Rest areas are open 24 hours a day, every day of the year, provide free parking (up to 2 hours) and toilets, and are accessible to disabled people. Other facilities, including fuel, refreshments, telephones, motels and tourist information, may also be provided but are not mandatory.

Signs may be provided to indicate that services are not available on the motorway.

No services on motorway

Sign on motorway indicating that no services are available ahead. Drivers should leave the motorway if service facilities are required

No services on M 41

Sign on all-purpose road indicating that no services are available on motorway ahead. The motorway number may include a compass point (e.g. 'M 41(N)') if services are available in one direction but not the other

Other signs on motorways

M1
The NORTH
Sheffield 32
Leeds 59

A route confirmatory sign is provided after most junctions. This shows the motorway number and the distances to the main destinations ahead

For Docklands follow M11

Where there are more destinations than can be accommodated on the direction signs at a junction, a sign such as this may be used in advance of the 1 mile direction sign. It advises drivers of the route to be followed (or junction to leave at) for destinations that cannot be accommodated on the main junction sign

Works unit only

This sign indicates a slip road that leads to a maintenance compound and is not available to the general public

No hard shoulder for 400 yards

Where a motorway has been widened but the original bridges retained, there may be no hard shoulder under or over the bridge. Where this occurs, signs will indicate the distance over which this applies. There will be hatched markings on the hard shoulder at the point where it comes to an end

Authorised vehicles only

Observation platforms are sometimes provided at the back of the hard shoulder. These are reserved for authorised vehicles, such as National Highways traffic officers, maintenance vehicles or the police

HERTFORDSHIRE

County boundary sign (may be varied to show the name of a river)

Marker posts, located at the back of the hard shoulder at approximately 100-metre intervals, show the direction to the nearest emergency telephone (housed in an orange box). You can use the telephone to contact the control centre in case of an emergency or breakdown

Keep your distance

Some motorways may have special chevron markings in the centre of the traffic lanes. These are spaced 40 metres apart, and keeping two marks between your vehicle and the one in front will provide a safe driving distance at 70 mph. There will be signs advising you to check your distance, keep two chevrons apart and keep your distance.

Keep apart 2 chevrons

Central reservation

Check your distance

Direction signs for drivers of goods vehicles

Direction of route recommended for goods vehicles

This sign is located before the 1 mile advance sign for a junction ahead. It is used where it is not practicable to sign a goods vehicle route at the junction itself

Signs indicating the end of motorway regulations

Sign located at the entrance to a service area accessed directly from the motorway, or a maintenance compound

Sign located on main carriageway to indicate the distance to the end of the motorway

Sign located where the motorway ends on either the main carriageway or exit slip road

Motorway signals and variable signs

These advise of abnormal traffic conditions ahead (e.g. lane closures or fog) and may indicate a speed limit or provide journey time information. Where variable speed limit signs are mounted over individual lanes or at the side of the motorway and the speed limit is shown in a red circle (see page 21), the limit is mandatory. Speed limits that are not shown in a red circle are the maximum speeds advised for the prevailing conditions.

Signals and variable message signs may apply to individual lanes when mounted overhead or, when located on the central reservation or at the side of the motorway, to the whole carriageway. They are normally blank but, when they indicate a restriction, the reason may not always be obvious. There may have been an accident ahead, so take no chances and obey the signals. When red lights are flashing above your lane, you must stop unless you can move safely to a lane where red signals are not showing.

Red lights flashing from side to side in pairs, together with a red cross, mean 'do not proceed in the traffic lane directly below'. These signals are mounted above the carriageway: there is a signal for each traffic lane. A previous signal may direct you into an adjacent lane (see page 105). More than one lane may be closed to traffic

Red lights flashing from side to side in pairs, together with a red cross displayed on a sign at the side of the motorway, mean 'do not proceed in the lane to which the sign relates'. A previous signal may direct you into an adjacent lane (see below). More than one lane may be closed to traffic

Where red flashing light signals and closure of all lanes are shown on a sign, the road is closed. You must not go beyond the sign in any lane or use the hard shoulder to avoid the road closure unless directed to do so by a police or traffic officer

Signals and variable signs above each lane of the motorway

Each lane has its own signal; each signal has two pairs of amber lights that flash from top to bottom. You should obey the signal for your lane

Temporary maximum speed advised for prevailing traffic conditions

Move to adjacent lane (arrow may point downwards to the right)

Leave motorway at next exit

Risk of fog ahead

Risk of ice ahead

End of temporary restrictions

Lane-specific signs and signals can display advice, restrictions and warnings that apply to individual lanes.

60 mph speed limit signs displayed

Move to right-hand lane arrow displayed

Red flashing light signals and a red 'X' on a sign identify a closed lane. You must follow the instructions on signs in advance of a closed lane to move safely to an open lane. You must not drive in a closed lane. A sign will inform you when the lane is no longer closed by displaying a speed limit or the word 'END'.

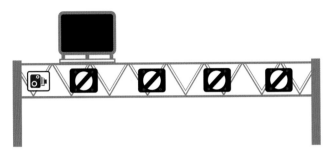

National speed limit applies after the incident

Signals and variable signs at the side of the motorway

These apply to the carriageway as a whole and are either located on the central reservation or mounted above the hard shoulder in combination with variable signs that display information about road works, congestion and diversions ahead. The amber lights flash in pairs from top to bottom

Various lane closures (signs for carriageways with four, three or two lanes)

Temporary maximum speed advised

Leave motorway at next exit

Risk of fog ahead

Risk of ice ahead

End of temporary restrictions

A single sign or signal can display advice, restrictions and warnings for all lanes.

60 mph speed limit with warning of a lane closure ahead

You should move out of the left lane and must not exceed 50 mph

Red flashing light signals and a red 'X' on a sign identify a closed lane. You must not drive in a closed lane. You must not exceed 40 mph in advance of the incident

End of lane closure and speed limit after incident

Signals and variable signs at the entrance to a motorway

All lanes closed (signs for carriageways with four, three or two lanes). Do not enter the motorway when the red lights are flashing in pairs from side to side

Older type of motorway signal

On some motorways, particularly in Scotland, you may encounter this type of signal mounted at the side of the carriageway. Flashing amber lights indicate that there is a hazard ahead. You should not exceed a speed of 30 mph until you have passed this hazard

Stopping on a motorway

If you need to stop in an emergency on a motorway with no hard shoulder, you should use the emergency area whenever possible. These are spaced regularly and are painted orange. Blue signs featuring an SOS telephone symbol indicate the distance to the next emergency area.

Emergency area

Sign indicating distance to next emergency area

If you need to stop in an emergency on a motorway with a hard shoulder, pull into an emergency area or move left onto a hard shoulder and try to stop near an emergency telephone.

Keep well away from your vehicle and moving traffic

To rejoin the carriageway after stopping from

- an emergency area, you must use the emergency telephone provided and follow the operator's advice for exiting the emergency area. A lane may need to be closed so that you can rejoin the carriageway safely
- a hard shoulder, build up speed, indicate and watch for a safe gap in the traffic.

Emergency area information sign

Direction signs on all-purpose roads

Junction ahead between two primary routes

Roads other than motorways are referred to as 'all-purpose roads'. Those of national and regional importance are called **primary routes**: they always have 'A' numbers. Direction signs on these roads have **green backgrounds**, yellow route numbers and white lettering. Primary routes, together with motorways, form a national network of roads between major towns (primary destinations).

Junction ahead between two non-primary routes

All other roads, including local roads with 'A' numbers, are called **non-primary routes**. Direction signs on these roads have **white backgrounds**, with black route numbers and lettering. Most road maps show primary routes in green and use other colours to distinguish between non-primary 'A' roads, 'B' roads and local un-numbered roads. Maps may also indicate primary destinations. The colour coding of these maps and the colours of the traffic signs may help you to plan your journey, using primary routes wherever possible.

Where a primary route has a junction with a non-primary route, a coloured panel on the advance direction sign is used to indicate a route of different status. Blue panels are used to indicate motorways (see page 92), green panels indicate primary routes and white panels indicate non-primary routes.

Sign on a primary route indicating a non-primary route

Sign on a non-primary route indicating a primary route

There are different types of sign that might be used on the approach to a junction. A 'map-type' sign shows the junction layout and is commonly used for roundabouts, with a special symbol for mini-roundabouts. The width of each route symbol depends on the type of the road indicated: wide for primary routes and motorways, medium for 'A' and 'B' numbered non-primary routes and narrow for local roads without numbers.

Map-type sign on primary route indicating a roundabout ahead

Map-type sign for a mini-roundabout

A stack-type sign shows directions at a junction ahead, but not the road layout. It can often be smaller than the equivalent map-type sign and is used for simple junctions (e.g. a crossroads) and where there might not be space for a larger sign, especially in urban areas.

Examples of stack-type signs. Arrows indicate the direction of exits from the junction ahead; each is shown on a separate part of the sign. The ahead direction may not be shown for a junction with a minor side road

A sign that indicates the appropriate lanes to use for turning movements at a junction ahead is sometimes used in conjunction with, or instead of, a map-type or stack-type sign.

Route numbers in brackets are roads that will be reached by following the route indicated. Where a primary route is reached by following a non-primary route, its route number in brackets is shown on a small green patch. However, non-primary routes reached along primary routes are not indicated on white patches. 'B 1234' in the example is a non-primary route. Signs indicating a route to a motorway include a blue patch with the motorway number in brackets.

Flag-type sign indicating a primary route that leads to a motorway and to a non-primary route

Signs located at a junction and pointing along a road have chevrons rather than arrows. They are called 'flag-type' signs. Some signs may be rectangular with upward-pointing arrows. These are used where the road divides, such as at an exit slip road or a forked junction. The background colour of a flag-type sign is that appropriate for the route indicated; coloured panels are not used where a primary route has a junction with a non-primary route. However, flag-type signs may include route number patches. A rectangular sign at the junction may have coloured panels, but only if it indicates more than one route.

Rectangular sign at a junction, indicating both a primary and a non-primary route. The background colour of the main sign is that appropriate for the main road on which the sign is located

Flag-type sign indicating a non-primary route

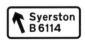

Rectangular sign at a junction, indicating a non-primary route

This sign indicates that a U-turn should be made at a roundabout ahead in order to follow the route to the destinations shown. It is normally located on a dual carriageway road.

Where a turning movement is prohibited, signs may show an alternative route

Direction sign showing distances to destinations

A sign may indicate the distance to a destination in miles. Fractions of a mile may be shown for distances less than 3 miles. Signs may be provided after a junction listing destinations and distances: these are known as 'route confirmatory signs'

Route confirmatory sign

Route confirmatory sign including a regional destination (The SOUTH WEST) and the distance to a motorway

Route confirmatory sign: Axtley is on the current route; Rickwell is reached by turning onto the B 1555 at a junction ahead

Route confirmatory sign on a non-primary route leading to a primary route. Lampton is reached by turning onto the A 11 at a junction ahead

Some junctions on dual carriageway roads may be similar to those on motorways, where a slip road leaves the main carriageway via a deceleration lane or a lane drop. The first direction sign on the approach to the junction is usually located ½ mile in advance, although there may be an additional sign 1 mile before the junction. In some cases, these distances may be reduced, normally to ⅓ mile and ⅔ mile respectively. Another sign will be located where the deceleration lane starts or just before the left-hand lane leaves the main carriageway as a lane drop. The signs may be mounted at the side of the road or overhead.

Signs located at the side of the road where there is a deceleration lane. The number of lanes through the junction remains the same

Where the junction ahead is between two primary routes, any non-primary route at the same junction is not shown on a white panel. Signs on the exit slip road will have green backgrounds

The junction ahead is with a non-primary route only, with the destination shown in a white panel. The signs on the exit slip road will have white backgrounds

This sign is located at the start of the deceleration lane. In addition to the side destination, the sign shows the ahead destinations

Countdown markers indicate the distance to the start of the deceleration lane. Each bar represents about 100 yards. These signs may also be used on the approach to a roundabout or crossroads. On non-primary routes, the bars are black on a white background

Signs on a non-primary route

A final route direction sign is usually located where the exit slip road separates from the main carriageway

Sign mounted at the side of the carriageway giving indication of a road layout at a junction ¾ mile ahead on a primary route, where the left-hand lane leaves the main carriageway and where the same exit can be accessed from lane 2

An indication of appropriate traffic lanes at a junction or at a junction ahead where the left-hand lane divides into two, with the additional lane on the left leading to a different destination (diagram shows colours applicable to sign on a non-primary route). The legend, traffic lane symbols and arrows will be white and the background green when the sign is placed on a primary route

Signs incorporating a 'Y arrow' are used on motorways and in other high-speed situations where a lane divides to reach different routes (diagram shows colours applicable to sign on a primary route)

Overhead signs for junctions with deceleration lanes and slip roads, where the number of lanes through the junction remains the same

Primary route sign

Non-primary route sign

Signs for a junction where a lane leaves the main carriageway to become the exit slip road. Primary route signs have green backgrounds. Non-primary route signs have white backgrounds

Signs mounted at the side of the carriageway in advance of the junction

Signs mounted at the side of the carriageway just before the left-hand lane leaves the main carriageway

Overhead signs

Signs for tourist destinations

Tourist destinations may be shown on separate signs with brown backgrounds, or on brown panels incorporated into other direction signs. See page 98 for tourist destination signs on motorways.

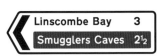

Symbols are often used to indicate the type of destination. These may be shown on road maps. Once the full name of a tourist destination and its symbol have been shown on a sign, subsequent signs may show only the associated symbol. Examples of symbols are shown below.

Tourist information

Castle

Historic house

National Trust

English Heritage

Theme park

Country park

Bird garden

Nature reserve

Farm park

Safari park

Beach

Museum (England)

Roman remains

Aviation museum

There are also symbols for sports and leisure facilities.

Football
ground

Cricket
ground

Sports
centre
(England)

Motor
sport

Golf
course

Race course

Fishing

Cycle hire

Ten-pin
bowling

Ski slope

See pages 121 and 122 for symbols and brown signs used for tourist facilities such as camp sites, restaurants and hotels. Some symbols are directional and face in the direction in which traffic turns at a junction. For ahead destinations, symbols generally face left. Some tourist attractions may use a general symbol, depending on whether they are in England, Scotland or Wales.

England

Scotland

Wales

This sign is used in advance of a junction, advising drivers of the route to be followed where it is not practicable to sign a tourist destination at the junction itself

Direction signs may indicate a route through an area of special interest

Signs showing the distance ahead to a tourist attraction

On the approach to a junction, a sign may indicate a town or geographical area with several tourist attractions

Location of tourist information point or centre

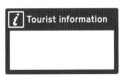

Tourist information board (sign for pedestrians)

Direction to a tourist information point or centre

Direction to a parking place associated with a tourist attraction

Services signs

See page 99 for blue-background signs indicating motorway service areas located on all-purpose roads. Services grouped together at a single location on primary and non-primary routes may be signed where parking, toilets, fuel and refreshments are available at least between 8 am and 8 pm on every day except Christmas Day, Boxing Day and New Year's Day. Signs on non-primary routes have white backgrounds.

Distance to services

Direction to services

'not 24 hrs' may be varied to 'Fuel only 24 hrs' or omitted if the services are open 24 hours every day. The cup symbol indicates that light refreshments are available. The vehicle and plug symbol denotes facilities for recharging electric vehicles are available

The services may have a geographical name. The 'LPG' symbol means LPG fuel is available, the spoon and fork symbol denotes a restaurant and the bed symbol indicates overnight accommodation. The truckstop legend indicates non-motorway services for goods vehicles only where parking, refreshments and toilets are available, and fuel may be available, at least between 8 am and 8 pm on every day except Christmas Day, Boxing Day and New Year's Day. Where the symbol has a red bar, services are not available for goods vehicles

Alternative signs indicating the entrance to services. May be used to indicate the direction to services at a road junction

Where individual facilities are available in a small town or village off the main route, signs at the junction indicate the direction in which they are located. If tourist facilities are available, the signs have a brown background and may include some of the symbols shown on pages 118 and 119.

Signs on the approach to the junction

Signs located where traffic turns at the junction

Brown signs may indicate establishments that provide restaurant facilities, light refreshments or overnight accommodation

Licensed camping and caravan sites, youth hostels managed by the Youth Hostels Association or Scottish Youth Hostels Association, picnic areas, viewpoints and parking places with tourist information may also be indicated by brown signs.

Camping and caravan site: the tent or the caravan symbol may be omitted, depending on the facilities available. The name of the camp site may be shown

Youth hostel

Picnic area: may include a name

Distance to a parking place with toilets, tourist information, picnic area, telephone and viewpoint. The symbols may be varied as appropriate

Parking signs

Direction signs indicating parking places, such as off-street car parks, have white backgrounds, even on primary routes. Where the parking destination is incorporated into a primary route sign with a green background, it is shown on a white panel.

The signs may include various details about the parking places.

Where parking places in different directions are shown on a sign in advance of a junction, the 'P' symbol may be shown at the top of the sign only

This map-type sign indicates the direction of routes to parking places from a double mini-roundabout ahead. The route to the right leads to a parking place for solo motorcycles only

A variable message sign may indicate the availability of spaces at each parking place. Some signs may show the number of vacant spaces; these are updated at regular intervals throughout the day

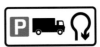

Where a parking place is for a particular class of vehicle, this may be shown by the appropriate symbol. This sign indicates a lorry park that is reached by making a U-turn at a roundabout ahead

Direction and distance to a multi-storey car park

Direction to a parking place that is available on certain days only

Direction to a parking place that has been approved by the police under the Safer Parking Scheme

Direction to a parking place showing the total number of spaces

Sign showing the facilities available at a parking place ahead. The lorry symbol is omitted where there is no restriction on the class of vehicle

Signs may indicate the location of parking places associated with 'Park and Ride' schemes. Where appropriate, the bus symbol is changed to another form of transport, e.g. tram, national railway or London Underground. The sign may include the name of the Park and Ride site or the place that it serves. It may also include the times of operation. Other direction signs may incorporate the blue 'Park and Ride' panel.

Signs for drivers of goods vehicles

Routes recommended for goods vehicles have black signs with a white lorry symbol. Other direction signs may incorporate black lorry route panels. The most suitable route for lorries to a particular destination may be different from that for other vehicles. The lorry symbol faces in the direction in which vehicles turn at a junction. For ahead destinations, the symbol generally faces left. Where route numbers for motorways and primary routes are shown, these are placed on blue and green patches respectively.

Direction sign at a junction

Direction signs on the approach to a junction

This sign is used in advance of a junction, advising drivers of goods vehicles of the route to be followed where it is not practicable to sign the route at the junction itself

Signs for traffic diversions

The symbol on this sign may be replaced by route numbers

Where, in an emergency, it is necessary to close a section of motorway or other main road to traffic, a temporary sign may advise drivers to follow a diversion route. To help drivers navigate the route, black symbols on yellow patches may be permanently displayed on existing direction signs, including motorway signs. On all-purpose roads, the symbols may be used on separate signs with yellow backgrounds.

Symbols that may be used to indicate a diversion route

Signs incorporating a diversion route symbol that is shown alongside the road number of the route that drivers should follow

Separate signs indicating a diversion route (may be permanently displayed)

Temporary diversion signs may be required when a road is closed for reasons other than an emergency, e.g. to carry out works.

Examples of other direction signs

The name of the junction ahead may be shown at the top of the sign

Signs may incorporate hazard warning triangles. In this example there is an opening bridge on the road to the right

Signs may incorporate prohibitory roundels and indicate alternative routes

Direction signs at the junction may incorporate warning triangles or prohibitory roundels. A distance plate indicates that the hazard or restriction is not encountered immediately

A road through a by-passed town or village leads back to the main route

Staggered crossroads on a dual carriageway road: the white panel with the red border indicates a Ministry of Defence establishment

126

Ministry of Defence establishments may also be shown on separate signs with red borders, arrows and chevrons. The background colour is always white, even on a primary route

This sign shows a local road with three junctions ahead in close proximity. The 'WC' and wheelchair symbols indicate toilets with facilities for disabled people. The 'H' symbol on a red patch indicates a hospital with A&E facilities (if there is no A&E, a blue patch is used). At hospitals with an urgent treatment centre (UTC), the 'A&E' legend is replaced with 'UTC'.

Local destinations, including a railway station and recycling centre, reached along a primary route

This sign shows both primary and local destinations that are reached along a primary route at a junction ahead. At some junctions, a separate sign might be used to indicate local destinations where this would avoid putting too much information on a single sign. In this example, the sign indicates that the primary route is a ring road

These signs are used where there are more destinations than can be accommodated on the signs at a junction. They are located in advance of the first sign for the junction and advise drivers of the routes to be followed for particular destinations

Signs may indicate an alternative route

Direction to an airport. The aircraft symbol usually points in the same direction as the arrow, as shown

Direction to a car ferry. The car symbols are replaced by the words 'Pedestrian ferry' when the ferry is for foot passengers only

Direction to a vehicle ferry. The car symbol is replaced by a second lorry symbol when the ferry is for goods vehicles only

This primary route sign indicates the directions to a ferry and an airport. It also shows a road to which entry is prohibited

The route to the left has a priority lane that avoids the roundabout (see page 82 for road markings). The route to the right leads to town centre parking and a railway station

Direction to a London Underground station

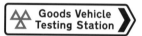

Direction to a Driver and Vehicle Standards Agency (DVSA) testing station for goods vehicles

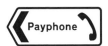

Direction to a public telephone

Direction to public toilets with facilities for disabled people

Direction to a 'Shopmobility' service for disabled people

A modern version of the traditional fingerpost may be used at some junctions on minor rural roads. The sign may have a square end and may include a distance in miles. More than one destination may be shown

Signs indicating the direction to a new housing development may be left in place for up to six months after completion of the development

Signs with a light green background and yellow border are used to indicate the route for emergency vehicles to a permanent incident control point

Signs with a red background are used to indicate the route for emergency vehicles to a temporary incident control point

Signs that indicate the appropriate traffic lanes for turning movements at a junction ahead may be used alone or in addition to map-type or stack-type advance direction signs. Signs on primary routes have green backgrounds, and signs on non-primary routes have white backgrounds

These signs show how traffic lanes on a slip road join the main carriageway of a dual carriageway road at junctions. Signs on primary routes have green backgrounds, and signs on non-primary route have white backgrounds

Sign for drivers on slip road

Sign for drivers on main carriageway

The slip road joins the main carriageway as a lane gain to increase the number of lanes from two to three. A distance panel may be added

Sign for drivers on slip road

Sign for drivers on main carriageway

The right-hand lane of the slip road joins the main carriageway as a merge with an acceleration lane. This is followed by the left-hand lane, which joins the main carriageway as a lane gain. Chevron road markings normally separate the two lanes on the slip road. The distance may be omitted

Direction signs for cyclists and pedestrians

Direction signs specifically for cyclists have a blue background and include a white pedal cycle symbol. Most are free-standing signs, but some primary and non-primary route direction signs may incorporate a blue panel indicating a route for cyclists that is different from that for other traffic. The cycle symbol may also be used on pedestrian signs where cyclists and pedestrians share the route (see page 133).

Primary route direction sign, in advance of a junction, indicating a route for cyclists

Non-primary route direction sign, in advance of a junction, indicating a route for cyclists

Where the route indicated forms part of the National Cycle Network, the number of that route is shown on the signs in white numerals on a red patch. Links within the network may be designated as Regional Cycle Routes: signs indicating these have white route numbers on blue patches. Some local authorities may have their own numbered cycle routes using different coloured patches. Where a cycle route leads to a national or regional route, the number of the route to which it leads may be shown in brackets. Signs may also include the name of the route.

Number of a national cycle route

Number of a regional cycle route

Sign showing the direction and distances (in miles) to destinations along a named cycle route forming part of the National Cycle Network

Sign showing the direction and estimated journey times to destinations along a named cycle route forming part of the National Cycle Network

Sign indicating two different cycle routes leading from a junction ahead

Map-type signs may indicate the route through a junction. In this example, the sign shows the route across an entry slip road. A sign may be used to direct cyclists to a signal-controlled crossing

Direction of a national cycle route

This sign informs you that you are following a national cycle route with the number shown

Signs indicating the direction to a parking place for pedal cycles

Direction signs for pedestrians generally have a blue background with white lettering and include the walking figure symbol. In town centres, especially pedestrianised areas, other colours may be used and the symbol may be omitted; these signs may also use different styles of lettering. Pedestrian routes to tourist attractions may have brown backgrounds and those for public footpaths green backgrounds. Signs may include distances in yards or miles. Some signs might include the estimated walking times to destinations.

Pedestrian and cycle route to a railway station

A public footpath may be indicated by a yellow waymarker. A blue arrow is used for public bridleways. The background may be of a different colour

Information signs

Information about the road ahead

Distance to the beginning of a dual carriageway road ahead

Dual carriageway ahead

A section of dual carriageway road begins directly ahead

Dual carriageway for ½ mile

A short length of dual carriageway road begins directly ahead

Motorway

Primary route

Non-primary route

These signs indicate the loss of the right-hand lane on a dual carriageway road or one-way street. The signs may be reversed to indicate the loss of the left-hand lane. The number of ahead lanes is varied as appropriate. The signs are often used at the end of a climbing lane and may include a distance (as shown for the motorway sign)

No through road for vehicular traffic

'No through road' sign incorporated in a street nameplate

No through road for vehicular traffic in the direction indicated from junction ahead

Route unsuitable for heavy goods vehicles

Narrow road ahead with passing places at intervals

Passing place on a narrow road

Unsuitable for motor vehicles **Unsuitable for trailers** **Unsuitable for wide vehicles** **Unsuitable for caravans**

Route unsuitable for type of vehicle indicated. In addition to the signs above, the legend may be varied to indicate other types of vehicles

Signs for lay-bys and parking areas

Distance ahead to a parking place

Location of parking place (may include an arrow to indicate the entrance to a parking area)

Distance ahead to a parking place with an emergency telephone

Location of parking place with an emergency telephone (may include an arrow)

Distance ahead to a parking place for emergency use only

Location of parking place for emergency use only (may include an arrow)

Boundary signs

Signs indicating county, town or village boundaries may include a crest or logo, a message of welcome, a phrase about a local geographical or historical feature, or the names of twin towns. They may be any shape or colour. The town and village signs may also include tourist attraction symbols and road safety messages. A speed limit sign may be placed in combination with a boundary sign at a village gateway (see page 90). Some boundary signs may include a photographic image representing a feature of the area. Other signs may show the name of a river, inland waterway, bridge or tunnel.

Hospital signs

Hospitals with accident and emergency departments or urgent treatment centres are indicated by red signs. The words 'not 24 hrs' are omitted when facilities are available at all times

Blue signs indicate hospitals without accident and emergency facilities

The route to a hospital may be indicated on direction signs by the 'H' symbol on a red or blue patch, denoting whether accident and emergency facilities are available or not (see page 127).

Signs for pedestrians

Stepped entrance to a subway

Ramped entrance to a subway

Ramped approach to a footbridge

Stepped approach to a footbridge

Direction and distance to an emergency exit from a road tunnel

This sign advises pedestrians crossing the road that traffic is one-way in the direction shown

Signs for vehicle checks

Temporary signs are put out when vehicles are to be stopped for an excise licence check or vehicle inspection. These signs may apply to specific types of vehicle such as goods vehicles or buses, and they may indicate which lanes to use.

Examples of temporary signs for vehicle checks

The type of vehicle indicated may be varied to a bus, or lorry and bus together

Police signs

These temporary signs are put out by the police to warn of potential danger or an accident ahead and the need to proceed with caution

In an emergency, drivers may be diverted onto the hard shoulder and told when to rejoin the main carriageway

Parking area reserved for police vehicles (the sign might say 'Police vehicles only') or additionally, when varied to 'Authorised vehicles only', vehicles such as those of National Highways traffic officers

Area where, from time to time, police carry out checks on the speed of vehicles

Signs for traffic surveys

SLOW CENSUS POINT | **CENSUS STOP if directed** | **STOP AT CENSUS POINT** | **CENSUS POINT**

These temporary signs are used when traffic surveys are taking place. Vehicles may be directed to stop at the census point

Other information signs

The depth of water at a ford may be shown in both metric and imperial units, or in imperial units only

Signs used where there are separate entry and exit points to and from a car park, private access road or private property

IN **NO ENTRY**

Signs for drivers leaving the public road

OUT **NO EXIT**

Signs for drivers joining the public road

Emergency access DO NOT OBSTRUCT

Where a road is physically closed part-way along its length to prevent its use by through traffic, this sign may be erected at the closure point. Vehicles should not be parked in a manner that would obstruct any gateway or opening that allows access for emergency vehicles

NEW ROAD LAYOUT AHEAD

A temporary sign may be provided for up to three months following a permanent change to the road layout ahead. The sign may be varied to indicate the nature of the change, such as a new roundabout, or that the operation of traffic signals has been changed

Traffic signals

In most cases, in addition to the primary signals at the stop line, there are duplicate signals, known as secondary signals, located on the opposite side of the junction. If the primary signal is not working, you must obey the secondary signal as if it were the primary signal.

RED means **STOP**. Wait behind the stop line on the carriageway until **GREEN** shows

RED and **AMBER** also means **STOP**. Do not pass the stop line until **GREEN** shows

GREEN means go **IF THE WAY IS CLEAR**. Take extra care if you intend to turn left or right, and give way to pedestrians who are crossing

AMBER means **STOP**. You may go on only if the amber appears after you have crossed the stop line or are so close to it that to pull up might cause an accident

Signals indicating a right turn

Although you may turn right on a full green signal, a right-turn **GREEN ARROW** showing at the same time indicates that turning right should be easier. Always check that opposing traffic has stopped before proceeding. If the full green is replaced by an ahead or left-turn arrow, you must wait until the right-turn arrow shows before you turn right

Signs may be placed with signals to qualify the meaning of the full green signal where movements through a junction are restricted

Signs may be placed with signals to qualify the meaning of the full green signal where movements through a junction are restricted

If a green arrow is shown with a red signal and the way is clear, you may go, but **only** in the direction shown by the arrow

Light signals for the control of pedal cycles (alternative types). **RED**, **AMBER** and **GREEN** have the same meanings as at other traffic signals

Low-level cycle signal may be used as a repeater or as an early release function mounted on the same post as a traffic signal or full-size cycle signal. It may be used on its own to signal segregated cycle movement

In addition to level crossings (see page 30), these signals may be used at other locations, such as lifting bridges, airfields or fire stations. When the **RED** lights are flashing you must stop. **AMBER** has the same meaning as at normal traffic signals

Tidal flow lane control signs and signals

On some busy roads, lane control signals are used to vary the number of lanes available to give priority to the main traffic flow.

Lane control on road leading from a junction ahead in the direction shown

Lane control on road ahead

Special signs explain what the signals mean

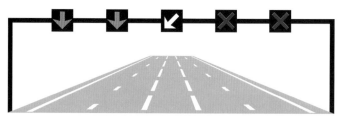

The lane control signals are displayed above the road to indicate the availability of the various lanes. A green arrow indicates that the lane is available to traffic facing the signal. A white diagonal arrow means that the lane is closed ahead and traffic should move to the next lane on the left. A red cross means that the lane is closed to traffic facing the signal

Alternative design of green arrow

Alternative design of white diagonal arrow

Alternative design of red cross

End of controlled section

Pedestrian, cycle and equestrian crossings

Zig-zag road markings

The zig-zag markings at crossings are there to ensure that drivers and pedestrians can see each other clearly. As a driver, you must not park your vehicle anywhere within these markings (before or after the crossing). Also, you must not overtake a moving motor vehicle within the zig-zag area before the crossing, nor must you overtake a vehicle that has stopped next to the crossing either to obey signals or because pedestrians or cyclists are using a zebra or parallel crossing (see page 148). If you are in a queue of vehicles that extends over a crossing, you should keep the crossing clear and look out for pedestrians who might be in the road. As a pedestrian or cyclist, for your own safety, do not cross the road within the area marked by the zig-zags: keep to the crossing. Crossings for cyclists or horse riders also have zig-zag markings, and the above rules apply to these also.

Puffin crossings

The puffin is a type of pedestrian crossing controlled by signals that can detect the movement of pedestrians, so that it can give them enough time to cross safely and keep any delay to drivers to a minimum. The pedestrian crossing time is automatically varied according to the actual needs of the pedestrian and, if after the push button has been pressed the pedestrian decides to walk away, the call is automatically cancelled and the pedestrian phase will not appear. This avoids unnecessary delay to vehicular traffic and the irritation that might be caused by stopping vehicles when no pedestrians are waiting to cross.

For drivers approaching the crossing, the signals operate in the same manner as those shown on page 140: there is no flashing amber signal as used for the older pelican crossing. If you are required to stop, do not proceed until you have a green signal and have checked carefully that the way is clear.

Near-side pedestrian signals with push button

The signals for pedestrians are located above the push button and are known as 'near-side signals'. They can be seen when pedestrians are facing oncoming traffic. If the green walking figure is showing, you may cross the road, but take care in doing so. If the red standing figure is showing, press the push button and wait for the green figure to show. Unlike in older crossings, the green figure does not flash before the signals change back to red. If the red figure comes on when you are about to cross, press the push button and do not cross. Traffic will still be held on red for those pedestrians who are already crossing the road when the red figure comes on.

Toucan crossings

Near-side signals for toucan crossing

A toucan crossing is used by both pedestrians and cyclists. Pedestrian and cycle signals are side by side and may be either near-side signals as for puffin crossings, or located on the opposite side of the road (far-side signals). The signals for traffic travelling along the road (including pedal cycles) operate in the same manner as those for puffin crossings (see page 144). Cyclists who need to cross the road will be directed to a cycle facility off the main carriageway, adjacent to the waiting area for pedestrians. Near-side signals include red and green pedal cycle symbols, together with a call button for use by both pedestrians and cyclists. These signals operate in a similar manner to those for puffin crossings. Far-side signals have both the green and red pedestrian signals, but only a green cycle signal. If the red standing figure is showing, either a pedestrian or cyclist should push the call button and wait until the green pedestrian and cycle signals show. Cyclists may ride across toucans, whereas they should dismount at other crossings.

Far-side signals for toucan crossing

Push-button unit for far-side signals

Equestrian crossings

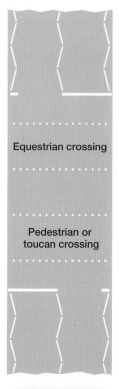

Equestrian crossing

Pedestrian or toucan crossing

These may be provided for horse riders where, for example, a public bridleway crosses a road. In most cases, there will be a parallel pedestrian or toucan crossing. The signals for an equestrian crossing use the ridden horse symbol and may be either near-side or far-side. Operation of the crossing is similar to that of a toucan crossing.

Far-side signals for equestrian crossing

Near-side signals for equestrian crossing

EQUESTRIANS
push button and wait
for signal opposite

WAIT

wait | cross with care

Push-button unit for far-side signals

Pelican crossings

Push-button unit

Far-side signals for
pelican crossing

Pelican crossings are no longer being installed, but many existing ones remain. At the end of the pedestrian phase, the green pedestrian figure flashes before the red standing figure shows. At the same time, the red signal for vehicular traffic changes to a flashing amber signal (replacing the red and amber phase shown on page 140). The significance of these signals is that pedestrians should not start to cross, but should continue if already on the crossing; drivers may proceed, but only if the crossing is completely clear.

Signal-controlled junctions

Road junctions controlled by traffic signals may include crossing facilities for pedestrians, cyclists and equestrians. The signals may be either near-side or far-side. You should press the push button and wait for the green pedestrian, cycle or horse signal to show. Make sure that all traffic has stopped before crossing. Far-side signals for pedestrians operate differently from pelican crossings. The green signal is followed by a blank signal: do not start to cross, but continue if you are already on the crossing.

Signalled crossings with central islands

Some signalled crossings may have central refuge islands. Where the crossings on each side of the island are in line, they operate as a single crossing. Where the crossings are staggered, they operate as two separate crossings.

Zebra crossings

Pedestrians should never cross the road within the zig-zag area. Drivers should stop at the broken 'give way' line (about 1 metre before the crossing) when pedestrians are using the crossing. You should give way to pedestrians waiting to cross and must give way when a pedestrian has moved onto a crossing.

Some crossings may be close to junctions where queuing takes place (e.g. at a roundabout). Drivers should not queue over the crossing and should take extra care when moving off, keeping a lookout for pedestrians. If there are two traffic lanes, but only one has a queue that extends over the crossing, drivers in the free-flowing lane should proceed with care and be prepared to stop, as pedestrians on the crossing may be obscured by stationary vehicles. You must not overtake a vehicle that has stopped at the 'give way' line to allow pedestrians to cross.

Parallel crossings

Parallel crossings are similar to zebra crossings, but include a cycle route alongside the black and white stripes.

Drivers approaching a parallel crossing should look out for pedestrians or cyclists waiting to cross and be ready to slow down or stop to let them cross. Drivers should give way to pedestrians or cyclists waiting to cross and must give way when a pedestrian or cyclist has moved onto a crossing.

Pedestrian countdown signal

Local authorities may install countdown units at traffic signal junctions and at toucan crossings, mounted either to the left or to the right of the green figure. After the 'invitation to cross' (indicated by a steady green figure) has been extinguished, the unit displays the number of seconds left to cross the road before the red figure will appear. This reassures pedestrians already in the road that they still have time to finish crossing.

Signs for road works and temporary situations

This sign, indicating road works or an obstruction in the carriageway ahead, may be used for any type of works, ranging from large construction schemes to minor maintenance

400 yds

M1 Northbound

Line painting

The 'road works' sign may have a plate that indicates the distance to, the location of, or the nature of the works

End

End of road works and any associated temporary restrictions, including speed limits

Barriers are used to mark the boundaries of an area of the highway closed to vehicular and pedestrian traffic

Traffic cones may be used to mark the edge of the route for vehicular or pedestrian traffic through or past a temporary obstruction

At night or in poor daytime visibility, road danger lights may additionally be used to indicate the limits of a temporary obstruction of the carriageway

national highways

Work starts here 21 July for 4 weeks

Delays possible

Major road works on M25 between J6 and J13

Delays possible

M4(E) Junction 16 to 15 Night closures Sat 11 & Sun 12 May

Signs may provide information about the location of current or future road works where delays or road closures are expected. This gives drivers the opportunity to allow more time for future journeys, use alternative routes, or make other arrangements for the duration of the works

On the approach to major road works, especially on motorways and dual carriageway roads, signs may indicate the nature and duration of the works

Signs for lane closures and contraflow systems on motorways and dual carriageway roads

The traffic lanes that remain open are available to all traffic. The red bar indicates a lane that is closed ahead

Some traffic lanes that remain open may have restrictions. This sign shows a narrow lane with a width restriction. Other restrictions may relate to the type of vehicle, vehicle height or weight

Traffic leaving at the next junction should use the near-side lane. This lane may also be used by traffic staying on the motorway

Traffic lanes divide ahead. The lane on the left leads to a junction and may also be used by traffic staying on the motorway. The right-hand lanes move to the right. Areas closed to traffic are shown in red

Traffic lanes move across to the left, making use of the hard shoulder. Drivers are guided by temporary road markings or yellow road studs

These signs show the distance over which the reduced number of lanes continue through the road works. The signs are repeated at regular intervals, usually every ½ mile. In these examples, there are no lane restrictions such as a width limit. The vertical black line indicates that the left-hand lane is the hard shoulder. The white downward-pointing arrow indicates a contraflow traffic lane separated by traffic cylinders (see page 153). Where the contraflow lane is separated by a physical barrier or a buffer lane (a lane closed to traffic), the white arrow is not shown

These repeater signs through the works are used where at least one lane has restricted use. The white downward-pointing arrow indicates a contraflow traffic lane separated by traffic cylinders. Where the contraflow lane is separated by a physical barrier or a buffer lane (a lane closed to traffic), the white arrow is not shown

Where a contraflow system operates, traffic cylinders are used to separate opposing flows of traffic in adjacent lanes

Junctions may be accessible from within the road works area. The sign shows an exit on the same carriageway. The style of numerals used for the route number depends on whether the signs are on a motorway or an all-purpose road. The black patch shows the motorway junction number

The hard shoulder is used as an exit lane at a junction

These signs are located where the exit route leaves the main through route. The upper sign is used on motorways and the lower sign on all-purpose roads

These signs indicate that use of the hard shoulder as a traffic lane has come to an end. Traffic is diverted onto the main carriageway. The sign on the right indicates that the carriageway ahead is fully open

Narrow traffic lanes revert to their normal width

Where delays are likely to occur at road works, the end sign may include a message of apology. The sign also means end of all temporary restrictions, including speed limits

This sign may follow the 'end of road works' sign to provide a telephone contact number for the traffic authority responsible for the road works

Temporary signs indicating lane priority at junctions

Where slip roads leave and join at junctions within a road works site, the permanent arrangement for lane drop, lane gain and traffic merge may be temporarily changed. Signs may be provided to show the temporary arrangements.

Sign for drivers on slip road

Sign for drivers on main carriageway

The slip road joins the main carriageway as a lane gain to increase the number of lanes from two to three. The permanent layout might include a traffic merge with an acceleration lane. A distance panel may be added at the bottom of each sign

This sign indicates a lane drop where the left-hand lane becomes the exit slip road. The permanent layout would be a lane diverge with a deceleration lane, with all three lanes continuing along the main carriageway

Signs for works traffic

Where it is necessary for works vehicles to gain entry to or exit from the works site itself, access may be directly from or to the open traffic lanes, such as a break in the line of cones. These entry and exit points are marked by red and white signs. Drivers should take care not to follow works vehicles into the site and to keep a lookout for vehicles leaving the site. These vehicles are likely to be moving more slowly than other traffic. Red and white signs may also be used to direct works traffic at road junctions.

WORKS TRAFFIC ONLY

Route to be used only by works traffic

WORKS ACCESS

Temporary access to a construction or road works site

WORKS TRAFFIC MERGING 200 yds

Exit from a works site 200 yards ahead

WORKS EXIT

Location of temporary exit from a construction or road works site

WORKS ACCESS ONLY 100 yds

Works access on the left, 100 yards ahead

← **WORKS TRAFFIC**

Sign to direct works traffic in advance of a road junction or works entrance

‹ **WORKS TRAFFIC**

Sign to direct works traffic at a road junction or works entrance

Convoy working

At some road works, other than on motorways, it may be necessary to slow traffic to a speed of 10 mph. To ensure the safety of both road users and the workforce, traffic is taken through the works in convoy. At the start of the convoy section, traffic is controlled by either traffic signals or 'STOP/GO' boards (see page 158). You must wait, where indicated, for the convoy vehicle that will escort you though the works. On single carriageway roads you must not overtake the convoy vehicle. On dual carriageway roads you may overtake the convoy vehicle, if it is safe to do so, after you have passed through the works area and signs have indicated that the speed limit has changed to a higher limit. Where traffic signals are used at the start of the convoy section, the red signal may show for a period longer than you would normally expect: **do not proceed until the green light shows**. Convoy working may take place at any time during the day or night.

Traffic control 400 yds

Traffic signals ahead where convoy working is in operation

Night-time works 14 July to 26 July

Expect delays

Advance warning may be given when delays are expected during overnight convoy working

CONVOY SYSTEM IN OPERATION AHEAD

Vehicles to be escorted in convoys through road works ahead

CONVOY SYSTEM TO PROTECT WORKFORCE

Reason for convoy working

WHEN RED LIGHT SHOWS WAIT HERE FOR CONVOY VEHICLE

Point beyond which vehicles should not proceed when temporary traffic signals show a red light

WHEN GREEN LIGHT SHOWS FOLLOW CONVOY VEHICLE

When the green light shows at temporary traffic signals, vehicular traffic must follow the vehicle escorting the traffic through the road works

CONVOY VEHICLE NO OVERTAKING

Sign on convoy vehicle ('NO OVERTAKING' may be omitted)

Mobile road works and lane closures

Some road works can be carried out without the need for road closures or major traffic management schemes. The area of work is protected by a large stationary or slow-moving vehicle with a sign mounted on the back.

On single carriageway urban roads with a speed limit of 30 mph or less, the works will always be on the near side in the direction of travel. A 'keep right' sign will be mounted on the back of the works vehicle or the vehicle protecting the works. There may also be a 'keep left' sign on the front of the vehicle to be viewed by traffic travelling in the opposite direction. Additional static 'road works ahead' signs may be placed at the side of the road and may include a distance plate such as 'For 1 mile' or 'Grass cutting for 1 mile'. There may also be 'road narrows on the left' signs (see page 11). The vehicle will usually have flashing lights on its roof. The type of work likely to be carried out includes grass cutting, weed spraying and gully emptying. On some busy roads, traffic may also be controlled by 'STOP/GO' boards (see page 158).

On single carriageway roads with a speed limit of 40 mph or more, the 'keep right' sign on the back of the works vehicle or the vehicle protecting the works includes flashing amber lights. These lights flash in pairs from top to bottom

On motorways and dual carriageway roads, mobile lane closures may be introduced on either the left-hand or right-hand side of the carriageway. More than one vehicle will be used to protect the lane closure. All signs will have flashing amber lights. A light arrow may supplement the white-on-blue 'keep right' or 'keep left' arrow, and flash alternately with the amber lights at the top

On the approach to mobile works on a motorway or dual carriageway road, vehicles with signs indicating the lanes that are closed will be on the hard shoulder or at the side of the carriageway. The type of work undertaken includes line painting, minor repairs and setting out static road works signs

Mobile carriageway closures may be used to convoy traffic when it is necessary to hold traffic back while cones and signs are moved to change a temporary contraflow system, or perhaps to remove an overhead cable. All lanes on the carriageway will be closed, but traffic will move slowly forward, over a distance of several miles, on the approach to the area where the work is being undertaken. By the time the convoy reaches this area, the works should have been completed, traffic will be allowed to increase its speed and traffic lanes will be opened. The convoy vehicles will have a large red cross and red lights flashing in vertical pairs

Temporary traffic control

At some road works sites on single carriageway roads where two-way traffic flow is not possible, it is necessary to alternate the direction of flow by traffic control. This is known as 'shuttle working'. For short lengths, this may be achieved by manually operated 'STOP/GO' boards at each end. At other sites, portable traffic signals will be used. They operate in the same way as permanent traffic signals (see page 140). Normally, a stop line is not marked on the road. A sign is used instead to indicate where you must stop when the red signal shows.

Portable traffic light
signals for the control
of vehicular traffic

Temporary signals
control a junction.
'3-way' may be varied
to '4-way'

Signs for an uncontrolled junction on a
road with shuttle working. The sign on
the right is for traffic on the side road

Temporary signals may be used to control a road junction. In
this case, the red signal is likely to stay on longer than for normal
shuttle working, as traffic on each leg of the junction will pass
through the road works separately. There may be a junction within
a length of road subject to shuttle working that is not controlled by
signals. Signs will warn drivers of this.

Miscellaneous temporary signs

Details of a new road scheme
under construction

Information about street
works, with an emergency
telephone number (sign for
pedestrians)

Maximum speed advised, in miles per hour, through road works

Temporary sudden change in level of carriageway

Risk of skidding and maximum speed of 20 mph advised on a road that has loose chippings

Sharp deviation of route to the left (right if chevrons reversed) at road works or other temporary obstruction

The end of a temporary mandatory speed limit is indicated by the 'end of road works' sign (see pages 150 and 154). However, the message may be reinforced by a sign indicating the permanent speed limit beyond the road works. This may be combined with the 'end of road works' sign. Where the permanent limit after the works is different from that in advance of the works, a speed limit sign is always used. The national speed limit sign shown in the example is varied to the appropriate limit

In the event of a breakdown within a road works site, await rescue by free recovery service

Instructions to drivers of wide loads on action to be taken before reaching road works ahead (instructions may vary)

Location of telephone to be used by drivers of wide loads to seek assistance

Additional traffic lane available ahead as part of a temporary traffic management scheme

Sharp bends ahead where traffic is diverted onto a temporary road for a short distance: the number of traffic lanes remains the same

This sign is used on a single carriageway road with more than two lanes, to indicate that a lane in the centre of the road is temporarily closed

SIGN NOT IN USE

Variable message sign ahead not in use or being tested

Traffic signals not in use

CROSSING NOT IN USE

Zebra, parallel or signalled crossing facility temporarily out of use (sign for pedestrians, cyclists or equestrians)

PEDESTRIANS LOOK LEFT

Temporary sign used at road works to indicate the direction in which pedestrians should look for approaching traffic

Temporary route for pedestrians

CYCLISTS DISMOUNT AND USE FOOTWAY

Temporary sign used at road works to instruct cyclists to dismount and use the adjacent footway

SLOW WET TAR

Temporary hazard: vehicular traffic should proceed slowly

WORKFORCE IN ROAD SLOW

Vehicular traffic should proceed slowly, owing to workforce in the road ahead

Vehicular traffic must not proceed beyond the sign when it is displayed for a short period during works on or near a road (hand-held sign)

NO HARD SHOULDER FOR 400 YARDS

Hard shoulder temporarily closed for the distance shown

NO ROAD MARKINGS FOR 2 MILES

Temporary absence of road markings for the distance shown

HIGHWAY MAINTENANCE

Sign on a vehicle being used in connection with highway maintenance works (flashing amber lights are normally mounted on the roof of the vehicle)

Miscellaneous signs

HOV lanes

HOV lanes (**H**igh **O**ccupancy **V**ehicle lanes) are similar to bus lanes, but they can also be used by vehicles (other than lorries) with at least one passenger in addition to the driver, as indicated by the '2+' car symbol. Where the requirement is for at least two passengers in the vehicle, a '3+' car symbol is shown on the signs. Solo motorcycles are normally allowed to use HOV lanes, but large lorries are likely to be prohibited. Signs indicate which vehicles are permitted in the lane. The aim of a HOV lane is to reduce traffic congestion by encouraging car sharing.

This sign gives advance warning of a HOV lane ahead

A separate sign gives the times of operation of a HOV lane ahead

Another sign indicates which vehicles may use the HOV lane ahead

Start of HOV lane (near-side)

HOV lane (near-side)

HOV lane road marking

End of HOV lane

Road charging

Road charging was first introduced in Durham and then central London. Upright zone signs for road charging indicate an area or network of roads where a road-charging scheme is in operation. Road markings may also be provided. The white on red 'C' symbol is used on signs to indicate such schemes. The symbol is also used to indicate congestion, toll or other type of road charging.

This example shows a typical zone entry sign. The charging period is shown in the lower panel. The name of the traffic authority may be shown at the top of the sign. The sign may be supplemented by a 'C' symbol road marking. Direction signs may incorporate the 'C' symbol to indicate routes that lead into the charging zone. Details of the actual charges and the method of payment are available from the appropriate traffic authority.

This information sign for a tolled crossing shows the distance to the crossing in the top panel, the charging period and charge in the middle panel and the method of payment in the bottom panel. To help reduce journey times and minimise congestion, some crossings may be free flow and not have any pay booths. The name of the traffic authority may be shown at the top of the sign.

For more information about charges, visit www.gov.uk/uk-toll-roads

Clean air zones

A clean air zone (CAZ) defines an area where targeted action is taken to improve air quality and resources are prioritised to deliver improved health benefits. In CAZs, some drivers may be required to pay a daily charge to enter, or move within, a zone if they are driving a vehicle that does not meet the particular standard for their vehicle type in that zone.

The white on green 'cloud' symbol is used to indicate a CAZ. The four classes of CAZ are indicated by the letter (A, B, C, D) shown on the 'cloud' symbol.

Class	Vehicle type
A	Buses, coaches, taxis, private hire vehicles
B	Buses, coaches, taxis, private hire vehicles, heavy goods vehicles
C	Buses, coaches, taxis, private hire vehicles, heavy goods vehicles, vans, minibuses
D	Buses, coaches, taxis, private hire vehicles, heavy goods vehicles, vans, minibuses, cars; the local authority has the option to include motorcycles

For more information about CAZ, visit www.gov.uk/guidance/driving-in-a-clean-air-zone

This zone entry sign shows the name of the traffic authority in the top panel, the class of the CAZ in the middle panel and the period of operation and details of the method of payment in the bottom panel. The period of operation may be omitted if the CAZ is operational at all times. More details of the charges and payment methods are available from the appropriate traffic authority.

This advance information sign shows the distance to the start of a CAZ, the class of the CAZ and the period of operation in the top panel. The bottom panel shows details of the method of payment. The period of operation may be omitted if the CAZ is operational at all times. More details of the charges and payment methods are available from the appropriate traffic authority.

Ultra Low Emission Zone and Low Emission Zone in London

The Ultra Low Emission Zone (ULEZ) was introduced in London and aims to improve air quality by reducing the number of vehicles in London that do not meet emissions standards. Cars, motorcycles, vans and specialist vehicles (up to and including 3.5 tonnes) and minibuses (up to and including 5 tonnes) not meeting the ULEZ emission standards must pay a daily charge to drive within the zone.

The Low Emission Zone (LEZ) was introduced in London and is designed to reduce harmful emissions from the most polluting diesel-engined lorries, coaches and buses. Cars and motorcycles are not affected. Vehicles not meeting the LEZ emission standards must pay a daily charge to drive within the zone.

For more information about ULEZ and LEZ, visit tfl.gov.uk

This zone entry sign indicates that both the ULEZ and LEZ are in operation. The name of the traffic authority is shown in the top panel. The charging period, if not applicable at all times, may be shown in a panel below the lower panel. Details of the charges and payment methods are available from the appropriate traffic authority.

This advance information sign shows the distance to the start of the LEZ and ULEZ zones. Details of the charges and payment methods are available from the appropriate traffic authority.

Low Emission Zones in Scotland

Low Emission Zones (LEZ) have been introduced in several Scottish cities to contribute to a reduction in harmful air pollution.

A vehicle will be in contravention of Scottish LEZ requirements if it does not meet the emission standard (unless it is exempt). Driving a vehicle in contravention of requirements within a LEZ in Scotland is not permitted.

For more information on LEZ in Scotland, visit lowemissionzones.scot

Entrance to a Low Emission Zone in Scotland

Direction sign showing the distance to the start of a Low Emission Zone in Scotland

Road marking indicating the commencement of a Low Emission Zone in Scotland

Advance notification sign showing the distance to the start of a Low Emission Zone in Scotland

Reminder to drivers within a Low Emission Zone in Scotland in which cameras are used to enforce traffic regulations

Rising bollards

In some town and city centres, certain streets may be closed for part of the day, either to all traffic (e.g. pedestrian zones) or to through traffic, with access permitted, for example, to public transport. Enforcement of these restrictions may be by the use of automatic bollards that rise from the ground to provide a physical closure.

Where such bollards are in use, warning signs are normally provided. Where certain vehicles are allowed entry, red and green signals control the operation of the bollards. Only one vehicle should pass at any one time and may proceed only if the green signal is showing. Some vehicles, e.g. buses, have devices that can be recognised by detectors controlling the operation of the bollards. If you are not driving an authorised vehicle, do not follow the vehicle in front, as you may risk personal injury and damage to your own vehicle. Where pedal cycles are exempt, a separate route avoiding the bollards is normally provided.

When illuminated, the red signal indicates the period during which an automatic bollard is in the raised position and that vehicular traffic must not proceed. The green signal, when illuminated, indicates the period during which an automatic bollard is in the lowered position and that vehicular traffic may proceed.

Rising bollards might also be used at the exit to a road-charging area (see page 163). These operate when payment has been made (similar to the exit from some car parks).

Driver location signs

These have been introduced at regular intervals along many motorways and some other roads so that, in the event of a vehicle breakdown or other emergency, the exact location can be identified quickly. They show the motorway or road number, the carriageway identifier and a unique locational reference.

Variable message signs

Some signs are designed to provide information about varying traffic conditions, such as delays or diversions ahead, or to warn of specific hazards, such as animals or debris in the road. These are called 'variable message signs' and may be free-standing with an electronic display, such as the signs that have been erected above motorway hard shoulders. Some direction signs contain variable elements. They might show, for example, alternative routes, or the availability of spaces in car parks.

Signs activated by moving vehicles are provided as a road safety measure. They can give a reminder of the speed limit, or warning of a hazard such as a bend or crossroads. They are activated when a vehicle is travelling above a certain speed and the driver needs to slow down.